ASK

ASK

BUILDING
CONSENT
CULTURE

Kitty Stryker

Foreword by Laurie Penny
Afterword by Carol Queen

Thorntree (🌳) Press

Thorntree Press, LLC
P.O. BOX 301231
Portland, OR 97294
press@thorntreepress.com

Cover design by HardestWalk
Interior design by Jeff Werner
Copy-editing by Amy Haagsma
Proofreading by Hazel Boydell
Index by Amy Haagsma

Library of Congress Cataloging-in-Publication Data
Names: Stryker, Kitty, 1984- author.
Title: Ask : building consent culture / Kitty Stryker ; afterword
    by Carol Queen ; foreword by Laurie Penny.
Description: Portland, OR : Thorntree Press, 2017.
Identifiers: LCCN 2017022470 | ISBN 9781944934255 (paperback)
Subjects: LCSH: Feminist theory. | Interpersonal relations. | Self-
    acceptance. | Mentally ill--Psychology. | Offenses against the
    person--Prevention. | BISAC: SOCIAL SCIENCE / Feminism &
    Feminist Theory. | FAMILY & RELATIONSHIPS / General.
Classification: LCC HQ1190 .S788 2017 | DDC 302/.14--dc23
LC record available at https://lccn.loc.gov/2017022470

10 9 8 7 6 5 4 3 2 1

Printed in the United States of America on paper that is Forest Stewardship Council® certified by the Rainforest Alliance.

Contents

Foreword

LAURIE PENNY

The language of consent has never been as vital or as political as it is today. Both in and out of the bedroom, we're far less free than we'd like to think. We're told that we live in an age of personal freedom and erotic abundance, but everywhere we look, an architecture of shame exists to strip individuals of their right to decide what happens to their bodies, to their lives, to our collective future. We need a new language of consent. What you're holding is a traveler's handbook for that new language.

Sex is where it starts, but when is anything ever just about sex? The overriding of consent has become not just a social norm but a mode of governance. We have a president who has groped and bullied his way to power, overriding the consent of the electorate just as he ignored the consent of the women he boasted of "grabbing by the pussy." We have a power elite perfectly happy to let him treat the voting public in the same way. And we have a backlash to women's push for sexual and social autonomy so profound, so vicious that it has congealed into a new sort of organized misogyny: people so incensed that they are no longer automatically entitled to women's time, attention, and sexual submission that they are prepared to create political havoc.

This collection is unique in that it makes the essential links between consent at the individual and sexual level and consent at the level of law, society, and governance. The strategies of political coercion learned and employed by the new right were first ritualized as a way of working around the new trend toward respecting women's sexual consent as a thing that might actually matter. The game playing, the gaslighting, the various methods of intimidation and taking by force the power and pleasure you feel entitled to by right of birth: this is how the new fascism operates at every level.

The rage that is rolling nationalists, misogynists, and white supremacists into power across the world is the rage of those who are prepared to tear apart the very fabric of civilization rather than face the possibility that women, queers, and people of color might have a right to agency. To autonomy. To dignity. It is the rage of spoiled children who hate to be told that they might have to earn their candy.

Over the past decade, the naming of rape culture in the popular imagination has been vital. Finally, we can understand that sexual violence not only is about isolated incidents of rape and abuse, but is an attitude that extends throughout culture, perpetuating and enabling that abuse. It's not just the frat boys who violate the freshman girl at the party—it's their friends, and her friends, whose first questions are how much she had to drink, what she was wearing, and whether she deserved it. It's not just the Hollywood star who abuses young girls for years with impunity—it's every aide, handler, and co-star who knew it was going on and said nothing, assuming that powerful men simply do these things, and why would you rock the boat?

Naming rape culture, however, is not enough. It was never going to be enough. The liberation of women, queers, femmes, and female-identified people is about more than negative liberty—it is about more than "freedom from." It's not just freedom from rape, freedom from abuse, freedom from fear. It is also "freedom to"—freedom to express desire, to explore pleasure, to seek intimacy and adventure. Perhaps what we should be asking of sexual liberation is not the mere absence of violence. Perhaps we should be going for something beyond "Let's not rape each other." What if we can do better?

I met Kitty Stryker at a fetish club in 2010, and it was Kitty who introduced me to the concept of consent culture—and who was, in fact, one of the first to articulate it when she bravely called on the kink community to clean its own house. The first thing she taught me is that consent culture is not about being "sex-positive" or "sex-negative." Those are worn-out ideas, requiring us first to believe that "sex" is a monolithic concept, something defined for us by patriarchy that we have to either accept or reject on terms other than our own.

That idea of "sex," the model of sexuality to which we get to say one simple yes or no and consider ourselves lucky if that no is respected, is male-coded, male-defined, painfully heteronormative, and entirely uninterested in women's pleasure. Sex, in this reading, is still something that men do to women, not something that people do together. Women get one choice—to let men do it to them, or to refuse—and whatever they decide is an invitation to punishment, to judgment. Slut. Whore. Bitch. Frigid. Prude. We can do better.

Consent culture is neither sex-positive nor sex-negative, but sex-critical. Consent culture demands a discourse of sexuality that allows women more than the bare minimum of autonomy.

Consent culture demands more of our sexuality than the absence of soul-crushing violence. Consent culture wants sex to be better—for everyone.

Of course, consent doesn't have to be sexy to be goddamn vital. Consent is sexy, but that, as this collection makes clear, is not the point. The fact that a shared lexicon of respect and autonomy opens up whole new vistas of pleasure and experience undreamed of by men-children frightened about not getting a fuck if they have to ask permission is not the point. It's a perk. A seriously decent perk, but that's not the point either. The point is the rewiring of hearts.

I truly believe that the language of consent is part of the slow growth of humanity toward its own adulthood. It is new, it is ambitious, and it can be learned, and if we are to survive this period of history we must learn it. It can be practiced anywhere: in relationships, in families, in communities— anywhere we think we can do better than violence and coercion. It is also, of course, about sex. It is about desire. But so are most of our politics, when you get down to it. I think we can do better, that we can be better, in bed and out of it, and this book is an exhilarating preview of just how much better it can be.

Fuck, yes. I'm into that.

— Washington, DC, January 2017

Introduction

KITTY STRYKER

This book has been a dream project of mine ever since I started consentculture.com. The consent culture movement and subsequent website were born in a dark room, watching *Born in Flames*, and drinking perhaps a little too much red wine. I was talking with a friend of mine about sexual assault in the BDSM community, and how, if we had a dime for every time we had been sexually assaulted as young submissive women, we would have a heavy enough sock to beat our abusers to death with.

That friend was unable to see the project through, but I am grateful to her for encouraging me along this path, in believing that I could help inspire something different. Something better. Something that took the consent part of "safe, sane, and consensual" seriously, while also recognizing and unpacking how systems of power complicate what we can say yes and no to.

I've spent a long time thinking about how I wanted to introduce this book to you, the reader. As anthologies go, this collection is just the barest brush against the surface of a topic that we should talk much more about. After all, consent culture is many complex things—I wanted to touch on so many areas of nuance. It's all so important, especially now, with a president who has blatantly and openly boasted about sexually assaulting women.

I realized it's now been six years for me of having tough conversations about consent, particularly as it relates to sex-positive culture. Founding consentculture.com was a process that led me to shift from identifying as sex positive to sex critical, embracing ideas from both sides of the sex wars in my ever-changing understanding of what consent is, and what it can be. I knew I wanted to contribute a book, an anthology of ideas, discussing consent culture...but how to make it different from what was already available?

I'm going to be blunt. Most books I found about rape culture and consent were written by and for middle-class, white, cisgender women. They featured the voices of more middle-class, white, cisgender women. As a middle-class, white, cisgender woman myself, I knew we needed something more intersectional. And as someone who has worked in the writing and publishing industry for some years, I knew I wanted the process of pulling together a consent culture anthology to display the consent culture values I championed.

My original pitch for this book was that this was going to be a book that talked not just about the issues around consent in daily life, but also what we can do about them—a friendly yet firm call to action. I was determined to make it accessible, moving away from being overly academic or needlessly hostile. I wanted a book where a diversity of voices could offer not just one solution but many. I have learned that there is rarely one right answer, and I wanted *Ask* to reflect that reality.

With that goal in mind, I required that my anthology signal boost the voices of marginalized people who are too often ignored in these conversations. To that end, I made calls for submissions available to non-white and non-cisgender people first, ensuring that I made room for them before anyone else. This also meant they had extra time to work on their pieces, a way of acknowledging that the hustle of freelance writing is often a more difficult balance for those who are not white and cis. I welcomed the writers to offer feedback about their contracts to ensure they felt the agreement was fair. My publishers, who feel as strongly as I do about this, worked with me to triple the amount we could pay our contributors. I made a point to reach out to the more marginalized writers to reassure them that they would not be tokenized. I made sure the participants knew that this was a conscious attempt to get the work of people of color, trans, and non-binary folks into the hands of white feminists—a group who needed to hear it the most.

At the end of the process, even with life complications meaning some dropped out and others took their places, I am pleased to say that ten of the authors identify as Black, brown, and/or people of color, and at least seven identify as non-binary and/or transgender. I wondered to myself after my experience: why do so many folks putting together panels, lecture series, books, or film festivals make achieving diversity seem so impossible?

Putting this book together has been an exercise in practicing what I preach around actively requesting consent, negotiating in nonviolent and flexible ways, and being gracious when called to task. I have no illusions that I am some sort of icon of perfect consent—I have crossed boundaries and hurt people in my life, and I'm sure I will again. What I hope to create with this anthology and with my work generally is a living demonstration on how to admit when a fuck-up occurs and how to pursue a restorative justice model when seeking to resolve conflict. There is no "right answer"—we are all products of our environment, and what feels soothing to me may be harmful to someone else. Instead, let us open our hearts to multiple paths, let us allow ourselves to stumble on the path, and let us work toward welcoming our callouts as reminders that we are still learning.

I want to take some space here to thank those who helped make this happen.

When this whole thing began, there was a lot of push-back from the "sex positive" community. I want to thank Jay Wiseman, who had my back from the very start, who supported every workshop I held and signal boosted my writing. You gave me faith that I was on the right path. I also have to thank the Center for Sex and Culture, which ensured I always had space for my consent culture workshops. Without it, this could've flickered out and died.

I have to acknowledge the risk my authors took in taking a chance on me and this book. Marginalized people are often asked for their labor with little if any return. I'm so thankful that the people contained in this anthology trusted me to give them room to speak their truths. This book and this move-ment are pushed forward by so many people, of which I am only a part. I'm glad I can highlight how this work is being done by such a diverse group of people in such a diverse variety of ways.

Ask: Building a Consent Culture benefits greatly from my ongoing education, thanks to the work of other activists and leaders. I particularly want to thank the radical feminists of color at Incite for their book *The Revolution Starts at Home: Confronting Intimate Violence Within Activist Communities*, which led me to ask more questions than I answered and made me aware of how much work is happening in margin-alized communities that never gets recognition. I hope this book helps to change that trend, even if just a bit. I have to thank Lisa Millbank of the blog *RadTransFem*, whose analysis of consent under white supremacy, capitalism, and patriarchy blew my mind and changed my understanding drastically.

And I can't forget the impact that sites like *Captain Awkward*, *Yes Means Yes*, and *Freaksexual* had on my framework.

I can't thank enough every friend who has come up to me and told me I'm doing vital activism. Every person who dropped off food on the doorstep, who gave advice on next steps, who helped me with my website, who cleaned my house so I could focus on the work. I particularly have to thank the Degenderettes, who have been a guiding light and a support system, and Poly Asylum, the Burning Man camp that gave me space to turn my ideas about consent culture into practice. I didn't really believe in community, but then I found mine, and it fills my heart with strength every day. Thank you for holding me in my radical vulnerability.

I am endlessly grateful to my wife for helping me edit my first book, for listening to me rant and rave and cry when it seemed too daunting. Thank you for feeding me and for helping me stay focused on my task. I am also grateful to my boyfriend for reminding me that there is in fact a world outside of my laptop, for the kisses and laughter that helped keep my heart light during this intense work. And of course I can't forget my fuzzy babies, Foucault and Nietzsche, who have taught me a lot about consent culture in how they communicate with me and each other. I am so lucky to have such a support system at my back, and I couldn't keep going without you.

I have learned so much from the writers in this book. Some of them are good friends and lovers, some have been teachers of mine, some I have admired from a distance. To be able to show this to you, the reader, as a project that is truly from the heart is deeply meaningful. I hope the pieces you read in here encourage you to ask more questions as you, too, help us build a consent culture. Thank you for joining us.

IN THE BEDROOM

Sex and Love When You Hate Yourself and Don't Have Your Shit Together

JOELLEN NOTTE

In my early twenties, young, searching for love, and with an undiagnosed mental illness, I heard the same words of "wisdom" over and over again: "You can't love someone else until you love yourself." Feeling like I was being asked to do the impossible, I spent a lot of time wondering what one needed to do to convince the world they loved themselves when actually doing it was unimaginable.

In my late twenties, my finally diagnosed but horribly managed depression coincided with a misdiagnosed, mistreated injury. The only thing everyone in my life at the time seemed to agree on was that I was so lucky to have my husband. I was living somewhere I didn't want to live for this man; I was constantly dragging my miserable, hurting self through everything for this man, while committing over and over again to "just try harder"—when I knew I was doing all I could just to keep breathing—for this man. I was dying inside, but wow was I lucky to have someone who would put up with me.

Years later, I'm dating online and very specifically looking for no commitments, no long-term relationships—I'm not asking for anything from anyone. My mentions of books like

Opening Up and *The Ethical Slut* bring all the poly boys to the yard, but frequently, my honesty about my mental health history sends them running, turning to yell over their shoulder the now cliché polyamory mantra "You have to get yourself together first before you can really 'do' non-monogamy!" I look around and notice how many non-monogamous women I know are concealing their mental health issues and facing struggles on their own in the quest to be the mythic "cool poly girl." I see a lot of women taking a lot of shit with a pasted-on serene smile because they want everyone to know they got themselves together and are now "safe" to be non-monogamous.

These examples from my own complicated history with both love and mental illness serve to illustrate problematic issues that exist on a larger scale. We, as a society, consistently tell people with mental illnesses that they are not eligible for love.

In our culture, we believe many things about the mentally ill: they are out of control, they need care, they don't have sex, and they are dangerous, but one of the most pervasive and dangerous beliefs is that they are incompetent. Additionally, people struggling with mental illness receive constant reminders that they do not deserve love/acceptance/sexual attention as they are, that they are less than, too much trouble, emotional time bombs who are too broken to give back what they take. As such, they need to try their hardest to act like they are "well" for everyone else's benefit, be damn grateful to be loved despite their brokenness, and not press their luck by needing too much. Working from these beliefs, we end up with situations like I've described above: people who happen to have a mental illness feeling sentenced to loneliness because they have a brain that doesn't let them love themselves first, "broken and lucky" mentally ill people who feel damaged and so lucky that anyone would be with them that they dare not question it, or the buzzkill mentally ill people who might "ruin people's fun" with their needs and thus feel it necessary to hide them. In all of these scenarios we see one common theme: the partner dealing with mental illness is set up to accept a lot of crap they wouldn't be expected to otherwise. All of these situations can lead that partner to surrender their right to true, enthusiastic, genuine, fully embodied consent.

Many people don't love themselves. They can't. They won't ever. Simply telling them they have to do that before they can have the love of anyone else not only is cruel, but can backfire dramatically. Knowing that self-love is the "golden ticket" to the world of love, sex, acceptance, and everything else we're told comes with it can lead to the sort of over-the-top, "I LOVE myself!" play acting that makes one extremely malleable and susceptible to the demands of others dressed up as sex and body positivity. Because after all, why wouldn't they want to do ALL the things if they LOVE themselves, LOVE their body? Right?! Acting out self-love doesn't leave much room for weighing real wants and needs, only for doing what looks like what the character that's been created—the one who LOVES themself so much!—would do.

The "broken and lucky" dynamic, which can be common in relationships where one partner does a lot of caretaking of the other, consistently sends the message that the mentally ill partner is "broken," that they are damaged goods, that they are "less than," and, as such, extremely "lucky" to have a partner at all. Once it's been established that the mere presence of the partner is a gift, every act of caretaking gets added to the relationship balance sheet, and the mentally ill partner is so far in the hole they could never get out. The balance of power in the relationship is completely out of whack, and here is where consent becomes problematic. This dynamic leaves no room for equitable negotiation; it's not a relationship of equals. One partner has all the power and the other—the mentally ill partner—is relying on them, is convinced they need them, and often feels they "owe" their partner so much that they have lost their right to differing opinions, desires, and needs.

"You have to get yourself together first" has become a polyamory mantra of sorts, and it's bullshit—ableist bullshit at that. What people are actually saying when they say this is "I got into this to have lots of fun sexy times, and your reality might get in the way of that, so please just be cool and sexy all the time." Allow me to be perfectly clear about this: one of the cruelest things you can do is to tell someone that they are ineligible for love because of mental illness. Yet this is something that happens all the time. In a discussion about this idea, upon hearing that I believed people who were dealing with mental illness should not face constant messaging that they aren't allowed to pursue relationships, an acquaintance launched into a vehement argument for the right of communities to exclude people who may be "toxic." Simply hearing the idea that mentally ill people should get love too made this person feel like he had to protect his community from the invading mentally ill masses. As he argued this point, all I could think was how people in this man's community must feel like they could not step out of line, have problems, or be less than fun.

The upshot is that the circumstances the folks living with mental illness navigate in order to feel worthy of love often require them to act "as if." As if they were healthy, as if their needs were being met, as if they were okay with things that they may not be okay with. There is a pressure to lessen the impact of your disorder on others, to shrink it down, and by extension to shrink yourself down. The less you that shows up, the less voice you have, and the less control you have over your circumstances. To the outside world you may look like a consenting partner, but when you only feel safe voicing one-quarter of your feelings, what is filling in that other three-quarters? Whose voice is that? Are you really giving your own consent, or are you simply giving the answer you know someone else wants to hear? The answer that causes the least trouble?

Going with the flow is not consent. Trying to be unobtrusive is not consent. Being afraid to bother anyone with your problems is not consent. Not wanting to cause drama is not consent. Not wanting to be a buzzkill is not consent. Not wanting your luck to run out with the awesome partner who is with you in spite of your mental illness is not consent. Not wanting the hot partner you've just met to think you're high maintenance is not consent. Hiding yourself to make someone else's life easier is not consent.

Yet we, in ways both implicit and explicit, ask the mentally ill to do these things all the time. The message is sent that certain people—cool, easygoing, fun people who don't cause trouble—are lovable, and that not fitting those criteria is inherently problematic, so those who don't should do something about it. Cover up that illness, don't let it show, and if it's too late, if we've seen it, have the good grace to be sufficiently grateful for any bones tossed your way, and then remember that you are on notice, on borrowed time, because you are lucky, and luck runs out, luck can be pressed, and you probably shouldn't press yours.

If we want to say "yes means yes" and make it mean more than "no means no," we need to go beyond the words to the lives that are shaping them. Someone who feels indebted to their partner, lucky to have them, in danger of losing them is not delivering the same yes they would to an equal. Someone who feels like it's not safe to show their true self, that they need to repress, hide, or stifle themselves lest they be cast out for being dramatic, may not say yes for the same reasons they would were they living out loud.

We can start to change this dynamic by changing the way we look at mental illness and the mentally ill. First off, understand that given the choice most mentally ill people would not be living with a mental illness. Working from that understanding, decouple people from their illness—your partner and their illness are not one; they are more like an ongoing wrestling match. Two entities locked together but separate. This new understanding allows you to see how you can enter the right to join your partner's team rather than stand off against your partner and their depression. Now you are working together. Rather than becoming your partner's adversary whom they have to protect themselves from or caretaker whom they are indebted to, you are their equal with whom they can negotiate. We need to stop infantilizing and desexualizing the mentally ill and start relating to them as competent people capable of making their own choices. This allows everyone to be open, honest, and communicative. People dealing with illness can enter relationships being truthful about it, and partners can join them as allies.

Genuine, enthusiastic consent is for everyone, and the pursuit of sex, love, and acceptance aren't limited to the healthy, but for too long, society has supported the idea that the mentally ill are unlovable. Let each other be where you are, love each other right there, tell each other it's okay to be where you are, and love each other even when you don't love yourselves.

The Legal Framework of Consent Is Worthless

AV FLOX

I keep hearing people say that consent is complicated. I don't think that it is. What is complicated isn't the idea of consent, but the framework we use to approach discussions about it and to understand our responsibility toward one another within.

Currently, when we talk about consent, what we're actually talking about is permission to engage in an activity, viewed as a legally binding contract. This legal framework results in static solutions, such as apps that require individuals who plan to have sex to sign an agreement that shows all parties are willing to have sex, for example. The problem with contracts such as these is that they ignore that things can happen during the course of an activity that change the willingness of a participant to continue, and that written agreements by their very nature may, in fact, create a vector of coercion for participants.

In addition, the legal framework of consent fails to account for the fact that people may enter into a situation where sex is possible without having decided that sex is an option they are going to take. We do this every time we go on a first date, and yet because we think of consent within a legal framework, we often end up seeing victims of sexual assault and coercion being reprimanded for dressing a certain way or accepting to go to certain places with an assailant prior to a rape. Many feminists have undertaken the work of educating the public to understand that what we wear or where we agree to meet isn't an invitation for sex, but because so many continue to operate from a legal framework, progress in this arena has been difficult. After all, under the legal framework of consent, when we agree to enter a situation where sex is possible, we are seen to be extending de facto consent to the possibility of sex.

Within a legal framework, our best option for avoiding consent violations is to stay home until we know with absolute certainty that we want to engage in sexual activity. This is fundamentally broken, and nowhere is this brokenness more obvious than in our many attempts to make it work somehow.

In 2014, California governor Jerry Brown signed Senate Bill 967 into law, changing the definition of consent on college campuses that receive State funding. The "yes means yes" law, as it has come to be known, spells out that for consent to exist, it is no longer necessary for any party involved in sexual activity to say no if they do not wish to participate. Under this law, all parties must give explicit, ongoing consent.

"Lack of protest or resistance does not mean consent, nor does silence mean consent," reads the addition to the California Education Code under Section 67386. "Affirmative consent must be ongoing throughout a sexual activity and can be revoked at any time. The existence of a dating relationship between the persons involved, or the fact of past sexual relations between them, should never by itself be assumed to be an indicator of consent."

Though considered a victory by its proponents, a number of students took issue with the law, on the grounds that consent is often granted nonverbally.

In a column reflecting on the application of the new law, attorney Hans Bader additionally warned that a State intrusion into relationships by means of forcing discussions of consent prior to and during sexual activity may violate students' constitutional privacy rights, under the Supreme Court case *Lawrence v. Texas* (2003), which struck down Texas's sodomy law, and federal appeals court decisions like *Wilson v. Taylor* (1984), which ruled that dating relationships are protected against unwarranted State meddling.

But there is another avenue where affirmative consent fails. Sometimes, while we may readily agree to engage in sexual situations, we may nevertheless experience harm during these situations that changes how we feel about what happened. Sometimes, these harms are things we're not immediately aware of, but which can and do still have a serious impact on our well-being.

For example, imagine I am with a person who has enthusiastically consented to a kinky session in which he has agreed to being tied up and beaten. During the beating, I employ a tool he likes that I am not familiar with, and the lack of technical knowledge about the tool causes me to strike in locations one should not, such as the less fleshy parts of his body where organs and bones are exposed. I am technically doing what we have agreed to, and despite the misses, the overall sensation may be sufficiently pleasant for him to choose not to end the session in that moment. However, once he is out of that sensory space and better able to reflect on what happened, it is possible that he will find the resulting damage impossible to overcome. Unfortunately, because he initially expressed enthusiasm for putting himself in that situation—perhaps even asking explicitly that I use a tool I was unfamiliar with and harbored reservations about using on him—he may feel as though he has no right to tell me he experienced a negative outcome, and if he seeks support, he may find that people's reaction is to question why he agreed to a beating in the first place, or with someone who didn't know what she was doing.

Without going into something like BDSM (which, it bears mentioning, isn't a protected type of sexual activity under U.S. law), consider the vanilla situation of a couple who, after enthusiastically consenting to making out, determine together that they wish to engage in oral sex and proceed to do so. One of them takes the other's penis in their mouth and begins to pleasure them. When the receiver of these attentions signals they are ready to orgasm, the giving party pulls the penis out of their mouth and masturbates their partner onto their own face. The receiving partner is on the brink of ejaculating and not capable in that moment of preventing the situation. After the pleasure of orgasm subsides, the partner who ejaculated on the other's face determines that while facials are a popular feature of pornography, the activity isn't something that they personally enjoy. What's more, they realize that they actually find the activity degrading to the recipient and the relationship, and are suddenly left to reckon with their feelings about their participation in it. Technically, both parties were doing what they agreed to do, and under a legal framework, orgasm could be argued to constitute a sufficient level of enthusiasm, which makes it difficult for this person to feel that they have a right to approach the other person about the negative impact that the facial may have had on them.

In a legal model, even one that attempts to expand our understanding of consent like affirmative consent does, there is no space for people to reflect on what they've done and honor the evolution of their feelings about it or about their partner in a wider context. This is because the legal model of consent is one that primarily focuses on whether static rules are being broken, rather than one that centers on the individuals, who are by nature dynamic.

There exists a legal avenue that attempts to address the way context impacts consent. Though limited, the notion of informed consent differentiates between assent and consent. In this model of the legal framework of consent, a person can express agreement to sex but still not be said to have given consent unless they are in possession of all the facts relating to the situation and to the other participant or participants.

Missouri is one of the few states that makes this distinction, and criminalizes what it calls "rape by deception." Under the Missouri law, "assent does not constitute consent if...it is induced by force, duress or deception." Kansas, meanwhile, criminalizes certain types of deceit when used for the purpose of engaging in sex. In Kansas, it is unlawful to knowingly misrepresent a sexual act as a "medically or therapeutically necessary procedure" or a "legally required procedure within the scope of the offender's authority."

In California, a 1872 law criminalized "rape by fraud," defining fraud narrowly as the impersonation of a woman's husband for the purpose of obtaining sex. This law was put to the test in modern times following the arrest of Julio Morales, who had crept into a woman's darkened bedroom after seeing her partner leave. The woman awoke to find Morales having sex with her, and believed him to be her boyfriend. When she realized that she was mistaken, she pressed charges, and Morales was convicted of rape for initiating sex while she was asleep (and therefore unable to consent), as well as rape by fraud, because he was counting on his victim to assume that Morales was her partner. An appellate court ruled that the law did not apply because the victim was not married to her partner; subsequently, this led to two bills being drafted to close this loophole to also protect unmarried women, which were signed into law by Jerry Brown in 2013. Morales was retried, convicted, and sentenced to time served.

Joyce M. Short, an advocate of general "rape by deceit" laws like that in Missouri, has devoted her life to lobbying for the passage of laws that distinguish between assent and consent. She had a three-and-a-half-year relationship with a man who lied to hide who he was, including that he was a married father of two children. To her and other proponents, knowing what act one is agreeing to is insufficient to give consent; one must also have the facts about the actor.

This tallies with laws around the disclosure of HIV, for example. As of 2015, at least twenty-four states have laws on the books requiring the disclosure of a known positive HIV status to sexual partners. However, as has been noted by human rights advocates, disclosure laws place an undue burden on people living with HIV, who face considerable stigma—including social, State, and employment repercussions—for disclosure of their status.

And what, exactly, constitutes "all the facts"? There are a number of things that people may believe relevant in a framework that requires fully informed consent, such as whether a person has ever engaged in sex work, or whether they are transgender. Given the disproportionate violence that sex workers and transgender persons face, it is not only reasonable but even adaptive for many of them to refrain from making these disclosures until they can ascertain that the person they are becoming intimate with is safe. The law cuts both ways.

Another way that we have attempted to acknowledge the way that context impacts consent is by toying with the idea that it should be possible to revoke consent after the fact. While this idea doesn't necessarily inhabit the legal framework of consent, the fact that we currently can't see consent outside this framework makes it trivial to dismiss.

As Kitty Stryker, the editor of this anthology, has written, "people say yes in the moment for a myriad of reasons—because they mean it, because they mean it at the time, because they're afraid of the consequences of saying no, because they've experienced trauma and saying yes makes them feel like they have some control over the situation because they don't think their no will be heard, etc.... We experience things in our past differently as we gain more information and grow as people—something that once made me angry might be funny years later, for example. Why wouldn't consent be similar?"

As Stryker notes in the same essay, this notion "scares a lot of people." She's right. As a general rule, humans do not enjoy uncertainty about things that may have a serious impact on our lives. The more we strive to ensure that we do everything in our power to behave in ways that minimize harm in our interactions with others and the more seriously we take consent, the more terrifying it is to feel like the signals we receive in the moment might be completely unreliable. But this is not because we believe people don't have a right to change their minds—no one is advocating that we criminalize friends who flake out on previously agreed-to plans. The reason we don't like this idea is that under a legal framework of consent, there is only one outcome for our failure, and that outcome—whether criminal, civil, or social—is punishment.

As a result of this, we make our focus not the feelings of a person who's been hurt, but the risks to ourselves. We become defensive, placing the burden of proof on the shoulders of a person grappling with the implications of harm they've experienced. Even as bystanders, we deny support to those who have experienced harm pending some form of official validation, such as an arrest or a conviction.

This is broken, and it's easy to see how our behavior here fails to match our behavior toward other types of wrongdoing that have become norms despite a lack of enforcement in a legal sense. For instance, cheating within a marriage may be illegal in twenty-one states, but adultery laws are so rarely enforced nowadays that most people don't know adultery remains illegal, or ever was. Norms around cheating have come to apply well beyond the institution of marriage, and now reach as far as to include violations of relationship-boundary agreements in polyamorous relationships. Today, someone whose partner has cheated on them or violated a boundary of their relationship is able to both advocate for resolution with a partner and in general access the support of their friends.

We do not need a legal framework to give consent legitimacy, and in failing to understand this, we are actively making it more difficult for survivors of consent violations to share their experiences and for communities to work toward functional solutions that actually address the problem. Because the legal framework necessitates punishment for "justice" to be served, it fails in actually creating a system for survivors to be supported, for harm to be addressed, for community interventions to prevent further harm, and for rehabilitation to occur for those who have harmed.

I firmly believe that we have made a mistake in accepting a legal framework in our analysis of consent. The well-being of people in our lives is not a legal matter, but an ethical one. We have the power to create norms that center on the experiences of individuals even as their views on these experiences evolve.

The most demoralizing aspect of our stubborn refusal to give up on the legal framework of consent is the way that the criminal justice system continues to show us, year after year, how ill-equipped it is to handle even the most egregious cases of assault, abuse, and other types of interpersonal harm. Over forty women have come forward against Bill Cosby, alleging that he drugged and raped them in a pattern spanning fifty years. Despite Cosby admitting to purchasing Quaaludes to disinhibit women, the statute of limitations on this crime makes conviction impossible. Brock Turner was caught red-handed assaulting an unconscious woman—he was tried, convicted, and given the equivalent of a slap on the wrist because the judge didn't want to hamper his future with a harsher sentence. These are two highly publicized cases. Most cases of interpersonal and sexual violence don't receive the same level of attention, and go unnoticed.

The trauma of reliving an assault in reporting it to law enforcement and in court, as well as the fact that most violations happen behind closed doors, making the other party the only witness, contribute to the overwhelming number of sexual assaults going unreported. In addition, it is a known fact that there are backlogs of rape kits in a number of jurisdictions across the country that impede resolution even for survivors of sexual assaults who report and have tangible evidence to present. According to the Rape Abuse and Incest National Network, of 1,000 sexual assaults, perpetrators experience no negative outcomes in 994 of the cases.

The criminal justice system fails again and again even for survivors who do everything they can to make it work. Despite knowing this, we continue to trap ourselves and one another within its paradigms. We must stop. Even if the criminal justice system were to take adequate measures to address its pervasive brokenness, there would remain a number of situations that make it difficult for survivors to advocate for themselves and find support.

We can do better. We must do better.

The Political Is Personal: A Critique of What Popular Culture Teaches About Consent (and How to Fix It)

PORSCHA COLEMAN

Like many in America, I was disappointed, but not surprised, when then presidential candidate Donald Trump was heard discussing in explicit detail the ways in which his power, influence, and money make it easy to sexually assault women.

It is jarring how we, as a country and as a society, got to a place where admitting to sexual assault can be explained away as locker-room banter to justify the offender being elected to the highest office in U.S. politics.

How did we get here? There is no doubt that lack of consent, rape culture, and making excuses for sexual assault are not new phenomena. These issues go back millennia, crossing the globe and touching societies modern and developing alike. An analysis of misconduct and popular beliefs about sexual ethos and consent across thousands of years and miles would take more space than this book offers.

What we can do is take a slice out of American popular culture over 2016 to 2017 or so, and take a hard look at the nuance and, more often than not, the *lack of nuance* that influences our conversations about consent—that is to assume that we are having conversations at all.

"Pineapples!" is Kevin Hart's hilariously yelled safe word in his infamous skit in the comedy special *Laugh at My Pain*. A safe word is a concept that started in BDSM and alternative or radical sexual communities as a way to ensure that both partners were comfortable with the activities taking place.

It is said that in every joke there is some truth; most people have been in an awkward or uncomfortable sexual situation and didn't have the language to say they weren't enjoying it or didn't want it to continue.

In a culture that falls heavily on the sword of sex just happening or "one thing leading to another," conversations about consent can range from blurry to nonexistent. Generations have been denied a comprehensive sex education, as dictated by religious norms, while being beset by media that accommodates the sexual fantasies of cis heterosexual male tastes, playing to a multitude of dangerous tropes and beliefs about sex and sexuality. This has created our current rape culture.

The Marshall University Women's Center defines rape culture as follows:

> Rape culture is an environment in which rape is prevalent and in which sexual violence against women is normalized and excused in the media and popular culture. Rape culture is perpetuated through the use of misogynistic language, the objectification of women's bodies, and the glamorization of sexual violence, thereby creating a society that disregards women's rights and safety.

While it is important to recognize that rape and rape culture affect every gender and not to dismiss those narratives, including but not limited to trans and non-binary individuals, the Marshall Center does a good job of creating a working definition of a very nuanced concept that highlights the need to create, grow, and support an environment of consent culture.

On the topic of creating consent culture, the Office of Sexual Assault Prevention and Response at Harvard University defines consent as follows:

- an ongoing physical and emotional process between people who are willing, equally free of coercion, communicating unambiguously, and sincere in their desires
- a mutual agreement to be fully present with one another throughout all interactions, to prioritize both yourself and your partners' needs, and to understand that someone may choose to disengage from the experience at any time
- knowing and feeling—without a doubt—that the other person is excited to engage with you in whatever activities you agree upon, regardless of whether the experience is amazing or mediocre

The concept that a woman's sexuality is wholesale available for men is one of the biggest underlying reasons that sexual assault is rampant and accepted. This reason is perhaps second only to the complexities of power and how power plays out in the patterns of assault, rape, and sexual misconduct.

I am reminded of two recent cases. The first one is Brock Turner, the convicted rapist and Stanford student athlete who assaulted an unconscious woman on campus and served mere months in jail, in large part based on being white, being male, and having class privilege. The other case that springs to mind is that of actor, writer, and filmmaker Nate Parker, whose acquittal of sexual assault came to light during the promotional period of his film *Birth of a Nation* and included details of him being verbally abusive to his accuser (who died by suicide in the years after the assault).

To compare the power a black man wields with the power that an upper-class, white male wields, even in terms of perpetrating sexual assault, is a taboo within many communities of color. The layers of cognitive dissonance that go into conversations about power and privilege in marginalized communities of color is staggering, though we cannot deny the impact that white supremacy has on the justice system and public opinion. It is worth mentioning, too, that Nate Parker has publicly and earnestly apologized, whereas Brock Turner and his family repeatedly deny any malice.

Nevertheless, these two cases of sexual assault, both on college campuses and both of which saw the perpetrators go virtually without punishment, speak to the haunting lack of ethics and consent that plague our society.

Much like the aforementioned safe word that Kevin Hart discusses in his comedy, alternative and radical sexual and spiritual communities tend to do a better job with teaching and expecting consent. This is not meant to imply that BDSM and alternative sexual communities are a utopia, because they're not, but one of the things these communities get right is acknowledging that the "just letting it happen" model of sex, sexuality, and relationships is detrimental.

There are many schools of thought to keep sex and sexual-based exploration safer that center on consent; among them are safe, sane, and consensual (SCC) and risk-aware consensual kink (RACK). These acronyms, and others like them, are calling cards of the kinky and sexually adventurous.

Because BDSM is part of a larger and more varied umbrella of spiritual and sexual ways of relating, seeing it come to the default world and enter the lexicon has been both amusing and concerning. On one hand, the default world can learn a lot about how to have better sex and relationships from many of the principles that are in place in these communities. On the other hand, a lot of the depictions of what kinksters and other alternative sexual and spiritual practitioners like me do avoid the very cornerstones that aid in creating discussion about better consent practices.

One of the most popular and most ridiculed major media depictions of BDSM as of late has been *Fifty Shades of Grey*, both the books and the movie as well as the countless pieces of merchandise, along with the TV specials and documentaries that have spun off from those.

For every safe word or other clear consent mechanism in mainstream media, there are dozens more examples of *Fifty Shades of Grey* and related material that peddle an edgy fantasy with little (or terrible) depiction of negotiations about boundaries and limits. We filter ideas that could help in tearing down walls of rape culture and sexual misconduct through the comfortable lens of what's already broken.

For many who are not members of alternative sexual or spiritual communities, the idea of adopting guidelines of consent from those communities may be unappealing or scary. Even with the abject success of the *Fifty Shades of Grey* books and movies, many want their "mommy porn" and "good old-fashioned smut" to stay well within the realm of fantasy.

Luckily, there are conversations about consent and systems of making consent more digestible that may be a bit more savory to people who do not consider themselves to be kinky, or who do not desire to take that particular path toward alternative sexual and sensual practices.

Popular sex and spirituality educator Lee Harrington devoted a podcast to the topic of consent, more specifically about new models of discussing and understanding consent.

Included in the conversation among the old standbys were a few newer options, and one of the most impressive and accessible of these was FRIES, which was coined by Planned Parenthood.

According to Planned Parenthood, consent consists of the following:

- **Freely given.** Doing something sexual with someone is a decision that should be made without pressure, force, or manipulation, or while drunk or high.
- **Reversible.** Anyone can change their mind about what they want to do, at any time. Even if they've done it before or are in the middle of having sex.
- **Informed.** Be honest. For example, if someone says they'll use a condom and then they don't, that's not consent.
- **Enthusiastic.** If someone isn't excited, or really into it, that's not consent.
- **Specific.** Saying yes to one thing (like going to the bedroom to make out) doesn't mean they've said yes to others (like oral sex).

FRIES is important, not just because it brings a clear-cut way to look at consent, but because it is bridging a necessary gap between the work being done to expand education and discussion about consent in default culture and in alternative sexual communities.

This gap in consciously thinking about our ingrained approaches to sex, sexuality, and how we handle sexual misconduct, rape, and assault are past due for some revolutionary upheaval. While I am not suggesting that everyone should go running to their nearest dungeon, I am suggesting that we take a close look at the healing benefits a new approach can have.

As a sexual assault survivor in my early twenties, knowing that there were other ways to walk through the world of sex and sexuality was invaluable. When default society passed along harmful messages that I was complicit in my assault, and when even I thought of and referred to the incident as "the misunderstanding," clearly there was a disconnect someplace.

This same disconnect is the one that leaves the gates open to downplaying assault as locker-room banter. Let's change the narrative.

IN THE SCHOOL

Rehearsing Consent Culture: Revolutionary Playtime

RICHARD M. WRIGHT

"Hey. Wassup? Can I talk to you?"

Nonplussed, she keeps looking at her cell phone.

"Hey. I'm talking to you. Wassup?"

She blankly swipes something on her phone, unfazed.

"Aaiight. It's like that. Cool. Well, maybe you will wanna talk to me when you see that I got video of when you jumped into the pool and your bikini top fell off."

A cell phone with the alleged footage gets shoved in her face. Her eyes widen, and she lunges for the phone, which is whisked out of reach with a sly "gotcha" smile.

"Delete that now!" she shouts.

"Ohhhh, you wanna talk to me now, eh? Well I ain't deleting nothing. In fact I'm gonna post it on Snapchat, on Twitter, on YouTube, on Facebook... You are going to be famous!"

"Aw, c'mon, no! Delete it! Please!"

"You really want me to delete it, huh? Well, whatcha gonna do for me then, hmm? You gonna have to be a lot nicer to me..." A lecherous gaze rakes up and down her body.

Pause.

She says "scene," and we shake off the characters. She becomes Tabatha, the co-facilitator, again, and I become Richard again. We look at the enrapt co-ed middle schoolers.

Tabatha asks, "Does that look or feel familiar to anyone?" Almost everyone groans "yes."

We offer the students a reprise performance, and this time we invite anyone to step in and join us to act out a creative and nonviolent solution to this scenario. Three preteen boys whisper excitedly to each other, then stand up.

"We'll do it!"

"Okay, great!"

Tabatha and I take a moment to go back into character, and then, action. We reenact the scenario, and in my peripheral vision, it doesn't really look like the boys are doing anything besides watching. We continue, and near the end, one of the boys approaches us, and addresses me.

"Excuse me, I need to ask you to delete that video."

I look at him with incredulous defiance.

"Why should I? I like this video."

"Well, because we used our phones to record you blackmailing her, so if you don't delete it, we are going to the principal right now."

My jaw dropped.

"Umm, wow! I guess I'm deleting this video!"

I'm half in character, half blown-away "actual me" as I mime deleting images from my phone. And, scene! We all applaud the boys for their creativity, for coming together as a small supportive group, and for using the same technology that was being used to cause harm to nonviolently de-escalate the situation.

When we checked back in with the youth, they reflected that it felt like they were watching YouTube, but that they could actually walk into the scene and directly interact. Everyone felt engaged, whether they were in the scene or watching their peers in the scene. They were ready for more. We had already warmed them up with interactive exercises, and their eyes were alit. Afterward, teachers even reported raised levels of participation in their students.

The methodologies that Tabatha and I use fuse the arts with our youth-mentoring skills, bystander-intervention techniques, and expressive-arts-therapy training. In February of 2015, I attended a particularly transformative healthy masculinity/bystander-intervention training with Men Can Stop Rape (www.mencanstoprape.org) in New York City, and the tools I acquired proved to be invaluable. Studies show that approaching youth with a bystander-intervention model is actually a lot more effective for reducing sexual assault, and it is also more enthusiastically received than programs that bill themselves as anti-rape.

We can tell youth that they are basically "rapists waiting to happen" (anti-rape initiative), or we can tell them that we know they would intervene if they saw harm happening to someone and that we want to help empower them to do that (bystander intervention). The kids jump in with both feet for the latter! It was amazing to see children (and young boys in particular) excited to do this work and engage their creativity with it. Also, studies show that not only do they go on to intervene, but they also do not go on to sexually assault people themselves. Bystander intervention also takes the onus off of the person being targeted to deter rape and empowers the collective to do something about it. It answers the question in the room when giggling boys are carrying an unconscious young woman upstairs at a house party, and people are not sure how to respond and are waiting for "someone" to say or do something.

Something that makes these techniques work is that it feels like play. And it is. Creativity-engaging, improvisational, revolutionary playtime. And like most structured playtime, like sports and games, while there is spontaneity and fun, there are also boundaries and rules. It is the boundaries and rules that ensure that people are treated fairly and that create a space where fun can be explored with more safety. In many ways, playing in safe spaces with rules that everyone agrees on feels like a tenet of consent culture. Practicing how to play a game well (without necessarily invoking a competitive spirit), can be thought of as one of the best ways to develop one's own relationship to consent culture, as well as to others in groups.

Children are typically responsive to games and playtime, but what about adults and their capacity for playtime? Sensual playtime? Sexual playtime?

Cuddle parties were started by Reid Mihalko and Marcia Baczynski in 2004 as structured workshops and events, and became a sweeping cultural phenomenon that spread like wildfire. On their website, www.cuddleparty.com, Mihalko and Baczynski describe a cuddle party as "a structured, safe workshop on boundaries, communication, and affection." As someone who has attended such a workshop, and even facilitated a few, I can share that beyond the images that may arise of people just hugging and cuddling all willy-nilly, there is a lot of work done around boundaries and consent before any cuddling happens. One exercise consists of simply practicing saying no to an invitation for touch. I say "simply," but at the same time it's not so simple, because it is a rehearsal to normalize saying no in a situation where someone may feel pressured to say yes (I'm at a cuddle party, after all; I don't want to be the one turning down everyone), and it normalizes receiving a "no" as something that isn't terrible or ego-destroying. It's just a no.

Consent is playfully and thoroughly rehearsed before engaging in touching and cuddling, and it's a beautiful experience.

To take things to another level of adult play and consent, I want to point to an exceptional online article, "An Essay on Consent, from a Woman Who Holds Huge Sex Parties," from www.huffingtonpost.com. This was an excellent and most thorough read on personal boundaries, consent, sex positivity, and sexual pleasure. Consent is outlined in several ways in this article, but two definitions stuck out for me.

The first:

> You must be in control of, and able to revoke, your consent at all times for that consent to remain valid.

Perfection. If someone gives consent, then passes out? Not valid. The author, Kate H., even went as far as to provide coaching for how to consensually gag someone's mouth during sex play, and STILL be able to get consent as sexual play continues. It's quite a masterful piece.

The other description titillated me, because it eroticized consent in a delicious, playful way:

> Enthusiastic consent is the most important concept in our community. Sometimes people say "sure" and they don't really mean it. (Which is why we use this instead of "yes means yes.") Unless you are certain that someone truly wants you to do that kinky thing to them, don't do that kinky thing to them.
>
> Pro tip: If you want to be really, really sure someone is enthusiastically consenting, ask them to say yes a few times before you do that kinky thing to them. Make them *beg* for you to do that kinky thing to them. Consent for the win!

How hot is that? No "maybe," no "ummm," just "OH GOD PLEASE YES YES YES!"

We can also translate this into everyday transactions around boundaries and consent. You are at a friend's house, and you see they have that book of Grace Jones' memoirs that you have been dying to read.

"Oh my God! You have this! Can I borrow it?"

"Ummm..."

"Please!"

While being excited about reading Grace Jones' memoirs is understandable, paying attention to cues is important. "Ummm..." is a boundary. It's not a clearly stated one, but it is hesitant. Steamrolling over it with begging, trying to wear down the hesitation, wouldn't be in alignment with consent culture. Enthusiastic consent, on the other hand, is what you would ideally want.

Take two:

"Oh my God! You have this! Can I borrow this?"

"Gurrrrrl, you *need* to read this! You don't even know!"

"YES! Thank you!"

That's more toward what we might love to aim for.

Much like how we have social norms around etiquette, consent culture may need to be taught from a young age, emphasizing empathy and consensual behavior during play-time and structured games, regardless of gender. We should be careful not to invisibilize the real impact of patriarchy, though, in an age where boys and men represent the over-whelming percentage of people who sexually assault others, where men who sexually assault women get a mere slap on the wrist, and where college frat houses ritualize rape culture with their own toxic "games." There may need to be repro-gramming that is enticing, fun, and affirming and supportive of our true empathic nature. Considering the fact that while most men do not rape, most rapists are men, it would be very important—no, essential—for men to model consent culture to other boys and other men.

We may need to plant new seeds that break through the ideal of the rugged individualist, and instead envision all of us belonging to a village, looking out for each other. And as children of all genders grow, consent culture "playtime" could become more adult oriented, until becoming sexually active has been prepared for with robust sex education and a strong foundation that values practicing empathy, listening to cues, and engaging in consensual fun. When we approach each other in this way as lovers, trust deepens. Doors to sacred sex may open when we honor the other's body as if paying petitioning at the gates to a sacred temple. We increase our capacities to love deeply, to see the other deeply, and to be seen deeply. Consent culture can be seen as a love practice, a practice of seeing all humans as sacred.

There are so many benefits to having a consent culture. Like all things that become a bedrock of culture, it will need to be rehearsed and practiced until it feels natural. I personally cannot think of many things that would be more beneficial and fun to practice.

The Power of Men Teaching Men

SHAWN D. TAYLOR

Before I can make the point I want to, it is necessary for us to have an operational definition of a word that I will use liberally throughout: power.

We hear it all the time. We talk about speaking truth to power. The concept of power dynamics comes up when talking about everything, from romantic relationships, to marginalized communities and the police, to inter-class warfare. There is the dictionary definition of power, the social sciences definition, and our personal ideas, informed by our experiences. For our purposes, I want us to think about power as the following: the ability to get others to do what you want them to do through charm, guile, coercion, guilt, feigning ignorance, threats of violence, and/or actual violence. I also want us to think about power, always, as power "and."

Power does not exist by itself, nor is it self-generating. It is attached to a locus: that "and" I mentioned. It is power and race, power and gender, power and money, power and (undue) influence, power and sexuality, power and authority (real or imagined). And power is not one-sided. There is always someone on the receiving end. There is always someone who feels the full effect and weight of power.

When you have power, it is one of the headiest feelings you can have. To know that you can get things done with little to no resistance can make you feel unstoppable. When you can direct someone to give you something or do something for you, and with the utmost certainty you know that it will happen, you can feel almost intoxicated. Whether you exercise your power through body or voice, it should always be filtered through a layer of responsibility. However, the reality is that most people do not see (or acknowledge or care about) the link between power and restraint. It is a lack of restraint that allows power to become the bedrock of abuse.

Restraint is not only about holding back. It is about self-discipline and, at the risk of sounding archaic, honor. While I understand that the notion of honor is usually associated with both patriarchy and Eurocentric ideas of chivalry, it is time for us to embrace a new definition. Honor can and should be reframed as seeing and holding in the highest esteem the emotional, spiritual, and physical integrity of others. No matter whom. No matter what. Honor puts the brakes on power and provides the foundation for mutuality.

When you do not have power, it sucks. And, frankly, it puts you in a very dangerous position. When someone overpowers you, you are completely at their mercy. You are a target and they are some kind of deadly projectile. You cannot move, yet they are hurtling toward you. And when they hit, the damage can, much of the time, be extensive and long-lasting. I have been both projectile and target.

I am a six-foot-one, charming, and fairly muscular man. I have size, presence, and charisma, all of which I have used to get things done, and to get people to do things for me. I have coerced and I have threatened to achieve goals. I have used these traits to bully and intimidate. I have also used them to be the life of any party I attended. I was (and can be, if I choose to) the center of all attention. As I get older, I have been able to get a much better understanding of the kind of power I have and how I use it.

I am Black and have been on the receiving end of State power and the wicked combination of power and fear. I also have been at the mercy of my mother's power, her anger, and her confusion, and know the extensive and long-lasting effects of being the target hit by a projectile. A projectile whose only mission was to strike me. As with any type of collision, the hitter and the hit are changed. In my case, I tried to undo the effects of my abuse by using my power against others. I would never be powerless again. And I was good at it.

I got what I wanted, when I wanted it. And if it did not happen exactly the way I wanted it to, I became scary. I would yell and threaten and force others to accept the reality I desired. While I was never outright physically abusive, I was a master manipulator of emotions. My behavior, this disgusting display of power and patriarchy, and borderline abuse, became worse when I started dating.

If a woman rejected me, no matter how polite she was about it, I went off. How dare she not recognize how lucky she was that I was interested in her? Did I mention that the power in interpersonal power dynamics is always attached to ego and an inflated sense of self? When I was rejected—no, rejected is not the correct word—when a woman told me that she was not interested, it was a challenge to my power. It was a disrespect that I could not accept. It needed to be rectified. I would insult her and tell her that she would be worthless without me. The thing about power is that it is balanced on the most precarious of ledges. If the power were developed in an honest and sincere way, a simple "no" would not feel like a punch to the stomach, or a stripping away of something vital. Power and ill-developed masculinity are a lethal combination.

I had a friend, Thomas, and he and I would always go out and try to "pull" women. We'd go to amusement parks, clubs, and parks, and talk to as many women as we could. At the end of our excursions, we'd empty our pockets of the phone numbers we collected to see who had the most. He'd always win. He was handsome and funny, and women were drawn to him in a way that they were never drawn to me. He would be with a different woman nearly every day. During this time, when I was a junior in undergrad, I started to see things differently. I started to see myself, and the world, in a wholly different light—especially when it came to my relationships with women.

I started dating a woman, Lisette, and she was having none of my ego-based shit. She showed me just how full of dangerous shit I was. Long before it became a buzz-concept, Lisette talked about how power derived from fragile masculinity was toxic and abusive. One night we were making out, clothes flying here and there, just at the point of making love. She stopped me. She put her hands to her chest and pushed me up and away. I felt that cold rage course through my body. I tried kissing her again, but she pushed me away more forcefully this time. I was furious. I felt the old insults and belittlements rise to my tongue. But I stopped. I didn't follow my old patterns of trying to unbruise my ego. I looked at Lisette, and the way she looked at me made me feel as if something in me was wrong, was broken, ill-fitting. I asked her why she rejected me. I was not angry this time. I was hurt. Well, it could be argued that I was hurt all the other times too and that I used anger to mask it. She accused me of, basically, masturbating into her. She expressed that she felt used and that I was only after my own pleasure, not caring about how she felt.

She was right.

I never thought about how she felt, what she needed, and if she was enjoying our lovemaking. We got dressed and

I made the decision to break up with her. She exposed me too much and I did not ever want to see her look at me like that again. But she held me accountable and our relationship deepened. I asked her if she thought I was some kind of rapist. She emphatically denied this. But she explained that by not asking, by not seeking consent, I was rendering her invisible in an act that was meant to be shared between us.

Every time we made love after that night, it was on mutual terms. If I expressed wanting to make love to her and she said no, it was no longer an insult—despite it taking a long while for it not to feel that like one. She taught me how asking to touch her, to kiss and lick her, to enter her could be just as sexy as anything else. She taught me about her boundaries and what she was willing and not willing to do. She taught me how respecting the integrity of her body was showing respect to myself. She showed me how to be an honorable man.

I tried to share this with Thomas, what Lisette taught me, and he attacked me. He called me a pussy and told me I was weak. I tried to get him to understand. He was the only man I felt I could be vulnerable with, so I told him how embarrassed I felt that it took Lisette to show me that my behavior toward her was creepy and reprehensible. Wasn't this something I should have known already? He dismissed me as being soft.

About a week after our blow-up, I saw Thomas at a house party. He was trying really hard to pick up this one woman, whose name I've forgotten. She was obviously drunk. Sloppy drunk, and Thomas took full advantage. After a while I saw him leading her to a back room. I panicked. I followed them, and when I entered the room, her dress was pulled up, and his pants were down. He looked at me, smiled a huge smile, and nodded his head. "See? That's what I'm screaming. You want some of this? I'ma get mine, and you get it after." I looked at this young woman, blasted out of her mind, mumbling, her head lolling.

I told Thomas that what he was doing was wrong. That she was damn near unconscious and hadn't given him permission. "Bitch shouldn't have gotten drunk. She wants it. You saw how she was flirting with me." Seeing her so powerless, and seeing him almost basking in the fact that she was at his mercy, enraged me. I ran to him and punched him in the jaw, knocking him out. I found the woman's friends and asked them to go see about her. She got home safe that night.

I wasn't happy about hitting Thomas, but I didn't know what else to do. I was new to this whole respect/honor/ask/respect women's boundaries thing and felt responsible, somehow, to hold him accountable. Without the violence, it is men's jobs to hold men accountable for this type of behavior.

To build a culture of honor in our relationships with women, men need not be afraid to intervene when other men attempt to take what they want instead of asking for it. Men have to train other men that respect for women, their bodies, and their wishes is our collective default setting. And most of all, men have to redefine the idea of power coupled with masculinity. We have to show them new power relationships: power and respect, power and honor, and power and permission.

It is all about power. And the highest form of power is the power you can deploy to keep others safe.

The Green Eggs and Ham Scam

CHERRY ZONKOWSKI

When I think about it, teaching the content of consent is a hell of a lot easier than teaching the practice of it. The content comes easily. For example, here's a quote from Junot Diaz's *The Brief Wondrous Life of Oscar Wao*. The young goth chick Lola is talking about writing on the beach.

> I would sit in the sand dressed in all black and try to write in my journal... Sometimes other boys would walk up to me and would throw lines at me like, Who fuckin' died? What's with your hair? They would sit down next to me in the sand. You a good-looking girl, you should be in a bikini. Why, so you can rape me? Jesus Christ, one of them said, jumping to his feet, what the hell is wrong with you?

Pointing out the way her answer exposes the underlying assumption that her body is there for their pleasure—that's a cakewalk. But take it a level deeper and something very troubling for the classroom starts to emerge. Look at the number of question marks in that quote. The asking of a question already implicitly suggests a power relationship, that the person asking has a right to ask. That's why we preface a question to a stranger with a polite "Excuse me"—in essence apologizing before we ask if we have no claim on the askee. It's why small children love to ask questions when they don't seem to care about the answers: it's the thrill of agency, getting a big person to respond to your demand. It's why kids are onto the next question before you can answer the first, and why, when tired of the game, we big people respond by reasserting our power: Because I said so. Stop asking questions now.

This is why street harassment, like in the quote above, so often takes the form of questions. Why don't you smile? What's your name? What's your number? Each question a reassertion of the basic right of (usually) male demand, male authority. That's also why our girl Lola up there answers in the form of a question: turning the tables on the power dynamic at the same time that she exposes the implicit rapist assumptions.

This all makes me wonder, as a teacher, whether consent can ever really be taught in a mandatory class. No, for real. Because I can teach the content, but the practice is elusive. When I lob a question out there into the classroom, I am an authority that is demanding an answer. And often those who reply are the ones conditioned to comply. When I throw a question into the classroom, it sometimes hangs there, uncomfortably waiting to be answered, until someone speaks up—often a woman, clearly uncomfortable with the silence.

I find myself, as a feminist teacher, wanting to hear more women's voices in the classroom and yet also wanting to teach women agency by teaching them they don't have to answer the call of authority. I employ tricks to get around being in the position of nakedly requiring a specific student to answer and to try to get different people to speak. I assign student-led discussions, and I go around the room to have people share their ideas, allowing people to pass if they must. I try to repeat that every voice is valuable. But, in a way, I keep coming back to the idea that our culture is saturated with the concept of obedience, and to truly teach consent we have to rethink almost everything about the way power dynamics are taught. A lot will have to get thrown on the scrap heap. Even some stuff we love.

Like...*Green Eggs and Ham*. A number of years ago I wrote a sassy little S and M spoof of *Green Eggs and Ham*, and a friend drew an illustration of it that hangs proudly in my living room. It shows Sam I Am—now Dom I Am—proudly wielding a crop behind that other character—you know, the one who has no name?—who is bent over with a worried look on his face. Studying this picture over the years I have come to realize that *Green Eggs and Ham* is profoundly fucked up. It's rape culture! No, really! The phallic Sam I Am insisting on his ego and his pleasure and emotionally coercing the poor nameless character with a ceaseless barrage of questions: Would you like it with a house? Would you like it with a mouse? The other guy, identity erased and unimportant, is subjected to harassment until he gives in and "likes" it.

NO MEANS NO, SAM I AM!

People don't magically like foods after they've been harassed into trying them. It's time to start looking at the underlying messages about consent that we are teaching when we read children's books, and as much as I enjoyed the book at the time, I think *Green Eggs and Ham* needs to go on the trash heap of history. It's okay. We can still have *The Lorax* and *The Sneetches*.

There are all kinds of things we need to be aware of when we have power over others. Whether that power is as a teacher or a parent, we should always think about how we are teaching agency. This means that we not make children kiss relatives they don't want to kiss, or wear scratchy ugly pink nightgowns just because their grandparents gave them to them for Christmas. It may be that there are times when we as adults do need to exert power over children's bodies for their own good: to insist that they hold still while we clean a wound or to wear a coat when it's cold outside. But a sharp delineation needs to be made between control over their bodies for their own sake and for ours. If we do make a child do something, we should be ready and willing to answer *their* question of why—to give them that trade-off of agency. They deserve an answer to their question and for it to be a good one, so that they do not automatically yield their control over their body to anyone who presumes to have power over them.

I collect stories about how people practice consent resistance. One of the most moving came from a friend of mine who told me that she was at a festival, high as a kite, and watching fire spinners with wide-eyed amazement and joy. Some guy she didn't know came up and asked her to dance, and she said no—with no anger, anxiety, defensiveness, or apology—because she was high enough to not remember at that moment that it was her job to cater to male entitlement. He asked again, pressuring her: "Come on, why not? You'll like it." (You'll like green eggs and ham.) And she turned to him again with no defensiveness, but in that moment pure astonishment that he would even ask a second time and said, simply, "But I don't want to."

"But I don't want to"—which is all anyone should ever have to say, which shouldn't be that hard, which shouldn't have stuck in her memory as being an extraordinary occurrence that she should have the freedom and the ease, for once, to just say simply "But I don't want to." But the freedom to forget the larger societal structures that we are caught in WAS unusual and extraordinary, so much so that she will always remember it, and when she told me I knew I would too.

The man who asked my friend to dance jumped back from her, not saying it, but clearly thinking it, *What the hell is wrong with you?* And the answer, of course, is absolutely nothing.

IN THE JAIL

Responding to Sexual Harms in Communities: Who Pays and Who Cares?

ALEX DYMOCK

Recent social justice activism on sexual consent has increasingly been motivated by the relationship between consent violations and questions of achieving justice. As college campuses move toward "yes means yes" models of negotiating sexual consent and institutional responses to violations are increasingly on the public radar, sexual harms[*] are on mainstream media and policy agendas as never before. However, as has been well-documented, these efforts often lead to official resolutions that expand the prison industrial complex and provide only increasingly punitive "official" solutions to social problems. In turn, these solutions guarantee, even if inadvertently, that people of color and queer and trans people are disproportionately policed, arrested, and imprisoned. Perhaps in response to this rising tide of concern about sexual violence, the "sex-positive" rhetoric I saw develop around the

---

[*] I draw the term "'sexual harms" from zemiology (the study of social harm) to avoid the false distinction between the legal and often institutionally perpetuated harms of the criminal justice process and illegal interpersonal violence.

communities in which I was involved in my early twenties has given way to a more sex-critical discourse, which attempts to avoid the kind of equation of sex as a fundamental good that characterized earlier sex-radical activism.

While this activism is without doubt a major step forward, one major component of this shift toward communities' self-critical attitudes toward sexual ethics and politics is the question of the role of the State in the event of sexual harms. As a queer-feminist criminologist and zemiologist committed to decarceration and the eradication of State violence, I have been inspired by the organizing efforts and strategies of groups like INCITE! (www.incite-national.org) and the UK-based Salvage Collective (www.projectsalvage. wordpress.com), who seek to find alternative means to criminal justice to address interpersonal violence, particu-larly gender-based harms, within activist groups and radical community organizing. Drawing on anarchist politics, the brilliant and now seminal work of Ching-In Chen, Jai Dulani, and Leah Lakshmi Piepzna-Samarasinha, *The Revolution Starts at Home*, outlines in considerable depth a set of tools to address and respond to abuse within activist circles using the principles of transformative justice. This is the idea of addressing the offending party while avoiding criminal justice interventions, and addressing the underlying causes of the violence within that community simultaneous to sup-porting and providing justice for the survivor. When I first came across these documents, I was, like many, inspired by the idea of a DIY approach to achieving justice for those harmed and addressing the underlying structural causes of violence. Indeed, within my own community, a similar set of principles was put in place (a "card" system, with a "three strikes and you're out" mechanism for excluding abusers, as well as the opportunity for the person harmed to take part in a mediated conversation with the abusive party, and read-dressing the conditions in the community that might have led to the abuse).

Over time, however, I began to observe that although this important and socially transformative work was being undertaken by a range of actors within these communities according to capacity and skills, the vast majority of the care work involved in supporting the harmed party was undertaken by those who identified as women or femmes, often people of color or those from economically deprived backgrounds. While cis men would browbeat over the fine details of public-facing community policy, strategize over the exclusion of abusers, and often take on the role of orches-trating the exclusion, it was too often left to non-cis men to provide privatized emotional care or more practical domestic support. To quote Kathi Weeks, "to say that work is organized by gender is to observe that it is a site where, at a minimum, we can find gender enforced, performed, and recreated." Besides shoring up false distinctions between private and public forms of labor, at worst, the distribution of work in these communities around the event of sexual harms ends up reproducing the very hegemonies and power relations that permit those harms to have taken place. In many cases those hegemonies lead to survivors being gaslit, victim-blamed, disbelieved, or excluded from their communities altogether. However, this situation tends to be viewed as merely prag-matic, since unsurprisingly the majority of survivors of sexual harms are also those who are transgender, non-binary, or woman-identified, and the presence and assistance of cis men in such spaces would render them unsafe.

I want to join together the insights of transformative jus-tice activist efforts with those of Marxist feminists, who seek to resist the social reproduction that leads to the gendered and raced divisions of unwaged care labor. The resulting questions I arrive at are what role we should ask the State to play in responding to interpersonal violence and how—if the State is formally or informally involved—we can avoid the replication of institutional violence it is responsible for.

The questions of social reproduction and the gendered division of care labor are not new topic for feminists and queers, and in recent years have gained increasing attention in activist forums. Silvia Federici's seminal essay, *Wages Against Housework*, lays bare the ways in which heteropatriarchal capitalist social divisions are crucially supported by the reproductive labor of women. Social reproduction, the "renewal of a subordinated class of direct producers committed to the labor process" through surplus labor, such as domestic labor, or child rearing, provides a lens through which we can begin to apprehend the kinds of work at stake in responding to forms of sexual harm. In particular, social reproduction theory describes the efforts to regenerate the worker outside of the production process, which allows them to eventually return to it. In this context, it is not simply the ability of the survivor to return to forms of paid employment outside of the activist community that is at stake, but also their work *within it*. Whether this reproductive effort is affective labor in the form of psychical care that allows the victim–survivor of violence to return to productivity, or material labor in the form of providing a bed to sleep in, food, or childcare while they recover, this work is both disproportionately gendered and never waged.

By raising these concerns, I do not want to suggest that we return the task of redressing the harms suffered by victim-survivors to the criminal justice system. We know too well the costs both to survivors themselves and to those whom the system increasingly polices. What I do want to suggest is that at a first stroke, we make efforts to better support those who take care of survivors of sexual harm. One solution might be community fundraising to ensure that those who care take a wage for this work, which would even out the hegemonic power structures within these groups in turn, and provide some public recognition to those who do this work. This is not to say that providing a wage absolves the problem of the gendered division of care labor, however. The very notion of social reproduction as "feminized labor" itself naturalizes gender roles, whether it is paid or not. To combat this second problem, a potential solution is that cis men pay their dues as caregivers to those who provide that care, whether it is affective labor, such as simply being a good listener, or other forms of material labor, such as domestic chores. By recasting and deconstructing the gendered roles that maintaining a community requires, this may also do something to nurture a more explicit, less exploitative culture of consent in activist communities. It is not, of course, that affective and material labor involved in responding to sexual harms is itself "forced," exactly, but it prevents the increasing efforts to "privatize" such work and to "counter the forces that would naturalize, privatize, individualize, ontologize, and also, thereby, depoliticize it."

A second and perhaps more controversial strategy might be to make demands on the State that supporting survivors of sexual harms is a question of basic welfare. One of the most pernicious consequences of feminizing labor is that it relieves the State and capital from any responsibility for much of the cost of social reproduction. If responding to sexual harms can be seen as a form of social reproduction, we should be demanding that victim services are adequately funded, and that they work to address sexual harms in ways that most benefit survivors, whether that is funding provision for the material costs of surviving sexual harms, or the affective labor involved in providing emotional support. Such work is undervalued and underpaid, and increasingly subject to the flux of markets and politicization. In the UK context, the socio-economic context of austerity has led to services competing against one another for a "market share" of the paltry funding available, and it is often the most "visible" victims who are prioritized for support. Furthermore, some support for victims has been moved from outside the criminal justice process to being positioned within it, with support offered only as a result of a referral from the police. It is no surprise, therefore, that communities turn inward to respond to sexual harms. We need to contest and rail against this marketization, and work with victim organizations to improve their responses to survivors rather than isolate ourselves from them.

Responding to sexual harms within communities is but a mere example of the gendered and raced dimensions of public versus private activist work in practice, and I have provided only piecemeal provocations and solutions here. However, the refusal of unwaged care work necessitates a rejection of the gendered distribution of labor, and has radical potential to contribute to the fundamental meaning and production of consent cultures. At a grassroots level, making care labor a question of public rather than private work mandates "an interrogation of the basic structures and ethics that govern this work" that might shift the very foundations of conversations about the mythologization of social reproduction, and the shaky grounds on which it is conceived as "consensual." As a starting point, we need to keep asking the questions of these spheres of labor: Who pays, and who cares?

The Kids Aren't All Right: Consent and Our Miranda Rights

NAVARRE OVERTON

"You have the right to remain silent. Anything you say can and will be used against you in a court of law."

In 1989, when *Cops* debuted, I was only six. For the next few years, I couldn't go more than a couple days without hearing some other kid sing the theme song, an endless loop of "Bad Boys."

On the bus, the playground, and in the classroom, the song was everywhere, and so were the kids playing cops, reading other kids their rights on the playground.

By the time I was arrested at fifteen, I had already heard the Miranda warning hundreds of times. So, when the cop asked if I understood my rights, I said I did.

But I didn't.

Despite the ubiquitous nature of the Miranda warning in pop culture throughout my childhood, I still didn't understand what my rights were when I was arrested. The familiarity of the words created an illusion of comprehension. At the time I thought the warning was just a formal way of making a suspect know that they were being brought into custody.

To me, my "yes" meant that I understood that I was being arrested, not that I understood my rights.

And it's not that I didn't understand that I could remain silent; I didn't understand that doing so couldn't be used against me. Pop culture discourages invoking your fifth-amendment rights. Crime dramas routinely paint suspects who do so as being guilty—remaining silent means a suspect has something to hide. I thought that invoking my rights would be as good as admitting guilt.

So I participated. I answered their questions. I told them what I thought they wanted to hear. I was worried the truth wouldn't be believed. So, I admitted to the crime hoping for leniency. I just wanted to go home.

After a few days in a detention center, I had my day in court and was sentenced to six months in a juvenile facility and probation until the day I turned eighteen.

It would be a few more years before I would learn what my rights really were and what I could've done differently.

§

Despite the fact that the Miranda warning doesn't look like a consent issue on the surface, it is. The idea behind it is that no one should feel forced or coerced into giving statements that may incriminate themselves, and that if one is to give such statements they should be given freely, with an understanding of the potential implications of said statements.

In other words, informed consent—via the waiving of a person's Miranda rights—is necessary for police questioning.

But how can true informed consent occur when we are bombarded with misinformation and propaganda about the police, their intentions, and, in general, the workings of the criminal justice system at large? Mass media is of course the primary vehicle spreading this misinformation, sometimes in the form of cop shows that appear to be harmless entertainment but actually work to shape a warped view of the police.

These shows do this by painting the police as mostly good protagonists whose intentions are always to do good for their community, while simultaneously painting those who are the targets of police as mostly bad, whose intentions are selfish and stand to harm their communities.

But it goes farther than the mischaracterization of the actions of individuals. Through primetime TV and streaming services, Americans are also being fed misinformation about how the criminal justice system works. The system is placed on a pedestal of near perfection, where the "bad guy" is eventually caught and charged with a crime. On some dramas that also depict the trial, if the defendant is found not guilty, it is almost never because we are supposed to believe that they aren't; it is usually painted as proof that any failing of the criminal justice system is the result of it not being tough enough on crime.

With regard to the Miranda warning, these police dramas give viewers the impression that only a criminal could incriminate themselves. This results in large numbers of the public believing that our Miranda rights only stand to benefit those who are guilty. In other words, many Americans don't understand the significance of their Miranda rights.

At fifteen, I probably wouldn't have been able to fully understand what my rights were, let alone how to invoke them. Multiple youths having struggled the same has led to attempts to simplify the language of the warning to something easier for teens to understand. In 2010, the American Bar Association passed a resolution calling for the simplification of the Miranda warning for use with minors.

Despite this, using simpler language still isn't required when questioning minors across the nation. In a response, New York senator Michael Gianaris has proposed a bill that would standardize a more comprehensible version of the warning for underage persons taken into custody. The bill would force police departments to alter the warning to be comprehensible to those with only an elementary-school reading level. As it currently stands, most warnings used across the country are only understood by those who can understand language at a college level. This puts not only juveniles at a disadvantage, but also older adults who for various reasons cannot understand college-level language. It's another way in which the system fails to be just to under-privileged members of our society.

§

But is simplifying the language really enough to create a justice system in which consent to be questioned without a lawyer is always informed and freely given?

When I think back to the night I was arrested and imagine that the language explaining my rights had been simpler, I want to believe I would've understood, but what if I didn't? And what if, despite not understanding, I thought I did? Why isn't the onus on law enforcement to make sure that a person being questioned really understands their Miranda rights enough to waive them? Could it be that the system wasn't designed to be just, but instead to maintain and further the unjust system of privileges and disadvantages, keeping those at the top on top, and those at the bottom from ever working their way up? Because how could the criminal justice system actually be designed to protect all members of society equally when the system under which it operates doesn't do the same? The truth is that the criminal justice system of a society can never be more just than the society it is built to protect; it will always work to maintain the status quo.

A yes-or-no question simply isn't sufficient to ensure com-prehension of complicated processes and rights, especially when dealing with minors. Law enforcement should be trained to test for comprehension and fill in any gaps in understanding before allowing a person in custody to waive their rights.

In 2012, Andrew Guthrie Ferguson, a law professor at the University of the District of Columbia David A. Clarke School of Law, published a paper in *American Criminal Law Review* calling for what he termed "the dialogue approach" for giving the Miranda warning to suspects. The dialogue approach is exactly what is sounds like. Instead of law enforcement simply reading the Miranda warning and then asking if the person being questioned understands their rights, a conversation would take place in which the officer would ensure that the person understood all of their rights before allowing them to speak without an attorney.

But this wouldn't even be enough, because law enforcement cannot exist as a force that isn't coercive when it is militarized. When people fear for their physical safety, they still may not invoke their rights, even when they understand them. Sure, it's a step in the right direction, but to obtain true consent, all coercive elements must be removed from the situation.

§

When I think back to the night I was arrested and imagine that I actually fully understood my rights, I still don't know that I would've invoked them. I was scared and thought that remaining silent would make me look guilty. That's the message I received from all those crime dramas that played in the background of my childhood. I knew that asking for a lawyer would only make me look guiltier.

§

The onus should be on law enforcement to obtain informed consent to question a suspect without a lawyer present. Still, it might be a while before this becomes a reality. The truth is that until fundamental changes occur in society, our criminal justice system will never work toward justice, because the system is designed to place certain populations at a disadvantage to maintain an oppressive status quo. We need to work toward tearing down the oppressive system altogether; it is the only way there will ever be true justice.

In the meantime, we can implement community-based solutions to teach people their rights and how to invoke them. Holding workshops, passing out booklets, and having conversations about the Miranda warning are all ways that we can take care of the people in our communities and make sure that they understand their rights. We should also have serious conversations about the ways in which police dramas misinform us about our rights, the intentions of law enforcement, and what it means to be a criminal. Creating media in which the realities of the criminal justice system are exposed would also be a step in the right direction.

No one should waive their rights without first understanding them or consent to questioning without a lawyer present.

Just Passing By

ROZ KAVENEY

It was a party in the late '80s—I suppose it was probably the summer of 1987—and we were sitting together on some stone steps in someone's garden. She had draped her black shawl around both our shoulders for convenience, and somehow that had moved into our lips tentatively exploring each other's cheekbones and then our tongues in each other's mouths, and our hands...

I remember the feel of her shock of raven-black, lightly moussed hair against my cheek. Some of it strayed between my teeth, but that was not unpleasant.

"God, I love big girls," she said, as she reached up inside my loose top and stroked the top of my breasts. "You're so tall and round and strong."

"Oh, shit," I thought, because it suddenly occurred to me that she didn't know. I mean, I thought everyone knew, especially in that crowd...

"You do know...?" I asked, really hoping that she did. "Um...my past?"

"You used to date Ash and it went bad? You go out with that weird submissive redhead? You used to be a working girl and you went to Oxford? Sure, I know all that."

Her voice was slightly bored, slightly petulant—I was asking her questions, and she wanted to go on making out.

"No, not any of those..."

How had she known all of those things and not the other thing?

It was the '80s, and a lot of people didn't know the words...

"I'm transsexual," I explained.

She started back, a bit pale.

"You're a transvestite? You're a bloke?"

"Not anymore. Not for years."

"But you've got a thingy?"

She looked slightly ill.

"Not anymore."

She looked down at my breasts that she'd been so into mere moments before.

"Hormones and a boob job."

Her gaze travelled much further down...

"Look, it's okay if it's an issue for you. I thought you knew. I thought everyone knew. I am six foot four, after all."

She looked a little sad.

"It's just that...I really love big girls. But..."

No matter how out I was—and I've never tried to be stealth for a second—it turns out from time to time that people don't know I am trans. I really don't understand that, because I have never made any particular effort to pass.

I made the decision back when I transitioned in the late 1970s. I had seen too many friends obsess with their privacy to the point that they were limiting their lives more than their need to be safe dictated, and finding themselves ethically compromised in every working or emotional relationship that they had.

Like I said, I am six foot four and have big hands and feet, so investing in privacy seemed a bad idea.

Obviously, in an ideal world, people's past gender presentation should not be anyone's business but their own. People should not want to know, and they certainly should not care if they did. But in the world of the 1970s and 1980s, and to a pretty remarkable extent thirty-some years later, we were not and are not living in that ideal world. I entirely respect people's choice to be stealth, but that choice comes with baggage and consequences.

I sat with a trans woman friend who had fallen seriously enough in love with a guy that she felt that they needed to have The Conversation and, though she was pretty certain he was a good enough person to spend a significant part of her life with, nonetheless thought that, on the whole, it might be sensible to be somewhere in public when she told him, just because that might stop him trying to kill her.

I watched another friend who had got seriously involved, as a stealth trans woman, in lesbian street politics and lost every friend she had when she was outed—even people she had protected from legal consequences after a major street action. She even had former friends trying to get her fired from her job. Some of them feel shame now about what they did then, but far too late for that to be remotely relevant.

On the one hand, stealth often enables people to have the life they choose, and on the other hand, that life may literally be taken away from them at any moment if their enchantments fail them. On the other hand, trans lives, especially the lives of trans women of color, are always at risk anyway. My reasons for being open were in large part an expression of privilege, though that privilege also meant I couldn't be stealth, even if I wanted to, and have the career I wanted—there were too many people around in my professional and artistic world who had known me before.

None of which is directly about consent, you may say—but of course it is. There is the legal issue: in the United Kingdom, a number of trans guys, or at least assigned-female-at-birth people who presented as male, whatever the specifics of their self-identification, have been jailed for having sex with women who claimed, truthfully or not, that they did not know. As yet, no trans woman has been charged, but it may only be a matter of time, given the attack on us from the Right and from some feminists who ought to know better.

In a transphobic society, it is not just our lives that are at risk. It is also our liberty, and if we are unlucky and find ourselves in the wrong state and thus the wrong prison, a lot more.

Further, in a transphobic society, the cis lovers of trans people are at risk. There have been documented cases—not many, but some—of straight-identified cis men being battered to death by queer-bashers for having trans women as lovers, or subjected to criminal and social sanctions, both in the global North and in the South. The women lovers of trans guys have been subjected to brutality and to so-called "corrective rape." In countries where being lesbian or gay is stigmatized or illegal, homophobes are always going to include the lesbian or gay lovers of trans people—and both the lesbian and gay worlds can be staggeringly hostile and excluding to people they regard as capitulating to heteronormativity.

Specifically, my woman lovers have been mocked or told that "no decent woman" would ever want to touch them again. In the case of one woman—I was her first woman lover—she was patronizingly told, by more than one woman, that she should regard me as training wheels and that now she should move on to a "proper" lesbian relationship.

It's not just people's physical welfare or social embarrassment that is the issue. People with transphobic attitudes often have enough institutional power to affect deleteriously the rights of trans people and their lovers to education, health care, employment, and education.

In a world that is full of institutional transphobia—even an LGB world where this is true—loving, even having casual sex with, trans people is an issue that affects the welfare of cis people, and this potentially has serious consequences. This means that we have to—as a matter of necessity as well as ethics—regard disclosure as an important issue within the broader issue of negotiated consent.

This further means that trans people who are in stealth have to trust their potential lovers enough to compromise—potentially—their stealth status enough to take the risk of telling them. I know that that is a big ask—because it means that should they fall for the wrong person, the entire structure of their life might be overthrown in a second. It also means that their lives might be at risk if they have fallen for the wrong angry man—but if they have picked the wrong person, he might turn on them at any other point for any other reason. It's not as if someone who might kill you for being trans is not going to be someone who would kill you for other reasons.

One of the great myths of transphobia is that somewhere out there lurks a cadre of undetectably beautiful or handsome post-operative trans people who rule by deceit and seduction. This operates in absolute tandem with the belief that all trans people are utterly obvious and pathetic freaks—bigots never have any difficulty believing two absolutely incompatible things simultaneously. Specifically, people who think they know all about trans people, in a negative way, are perfectly unprepared to deal with trans people who are just ordinary. They also sometimes believe that they can detect post-operative trans people by a particular smell—the phrase sometimes used about trans women is "hibiscus and pus."

In all of these cases, and in political discourse among the Right and some feminists who regard themselves as progressive, the myth is that trans people, and in particular trans women, are predators. This applies irrespective of whether a particular person has or has not had surgeries.

There is a case, therefore, that disclosure to partners not only is safe, considerate, and ethical, but is one's duty to the community of which one is a part, which is constantly damaged by those tropes even when they are entirely untrue. It's further arguable that being absolutely open—if one is privileged enough to be safe from the consequences of that—is a duty, because it makes it easier for younger trans people, and trans people who have deferred transition for a variety of reasons, to come out.

Consent culture is not just about consent—it is about informed consent, and that means, perhaps, a level of openness that is not always what one would prefer or what is convenient.

IN THE WORKPLACE

"Ethical Porn" Starts When You Pay for It

JIZ LEE

With so much discourse about "ethical porn" led by those outside the industry, many fail to realize that the most frequent abuse is the simple fact that most people are watching porn illegally. Forget "ethical porn"—let's talk ethical porn *consumption*.

Millions of traffic hits

Though a handful of Torrent seekers will take pride in being Web savvy enough to scam what they feel they're entitled to watch for free, and file-ripping Robin Hoods believe they're liberating porn to the masses, the people who go the extra mile to break the law are not actually the industry's biggest culprits. It's everybody else.

Let's face it: free porn is easy. It's the first high-ranking page results on Google. You'd have to actively *dig* to find a paid site. With tube sites, there's no need to pull out a credit card, let alone register or log in. These days you don't even have to click through an age page, one of the main gates many pay sites employ to prevent underage users from gaining access. The high traffic on tube sites, most of which are now run by one monopolizing company, only serves to exponentially snowball the "free porn" Google rank.

Most viewers are oblivious and don't think what they're doing is wrong. Prevalent sexual stigma also feeds the need for a quick and no-strings-attached search. The shame of seeing an adult company listed on a credit card statement or the sheer acknowledgment of paying for something that so many assume should be free is also a factor leading to people being reluctant to spend money. The perceived value of porn says as much about society's outlook on sexual labor as the legal restrictions on sexual autonomy. Who could blame them? Figuring out where to go and what to click is not the priority for someone horny.

Despite more engagement with today's porn performers through social media sites like Twitter, the lack of media literacy around how porn is made leads fans to make a lot of assumptions. They see films like *Hot Girls Wanted*, a 2015 documentary that went out of its way to exploit the "porn star" narrative, finding the youngest women working in the most culturally taboo of porn sites. The film stressed that these "girls" are pressured to do more extreme acts for lower rates, through the saturation of Internet porn and hundreds of hopeful performers, all the while failing to acknowledge piracy's role in the bigger picture.

How can I be sure what I'm watching was ethically produced?

One of the most frequent questions I'm asked is "How can I be sure what I'm watching was ethically produced?" Without getting too sidetracked by topics of fantasy and film, marketing transparency, and performer interviews, or going right to the source via social media—all of which help discerning viewers better research their options—the simplest answer is that *paying for your porn* is the most direct way to ensure key ethical production values.

Here's how. Without a credit card processor overlooking distribution, there's no way to know for sure if basic labor rights took place. There is no 2257 affidavit to prove performers were of legal age, no STI test results, and no IRS W-9 forms, and there's certainly no model release form to ensure the people on film consented to have their image shared online. Unless it features a major star, most pirated content doesn't even include performers' names, let alone custodian of records addresses. There's a mountain of paperwork missing. Paperwork that, for better or worse, is designed to protect performers' rights and safety.

I should take a moment to add that like in any other industry, there are people—whether bosses, employees, or coworkers—who use power and position to their advantage. Working in the business has helped many refine their ability to assert boundaries, something that's vital in the work we do. Leaps and bounds have been made toward the betterment of our industry's workers, including Los Angeles–based organizations like the performer-and-volunteer-run Adult Performer Advocacy Committee and the industry trade association Free Speech Coalition. These and many others push advancements in performers' bill of rights, sexual health guidelines, and advocacy to combat racism and sexual abuse.

Piracy as exploitation

As a performer, the only time I've ever felt exploited is when my work has been pirated. When I sign a contract, it's between the producer and me. For someone else to assume that right feels non-consensual. It's also illegal and a breach of site usage and copyright.

The efforts to end abuse in porn will not be won by abolishing sexual media. It will be through a decrease in sex-worker stigma and the granting of agency and access, for performers and viewers alike.

There's something to be said about free porn and the lack of informed navigation for porn on the Internet, through which most people view explicit content. Pirated content is uploaded without context, and clips are stripped from their larger storyline, retitled with new and inappropriate (as in rarely matching the scenario) headers. Performers lose their names and are given incorrect ethnicities or ages. It's next to impossible to find the video you want to see—assuming you know what you want to look for and how to go about seeking it in the first place. As Shine Louise Houston once described it, tube sites are so domineering that looking for online porn is like stargazing during the day: all you're going to see is the sun.

Is it really stealing?

Piracy also hurts the profit margins that allow performers and producers to keep making work. As a performer, I subsidize my income with affiliate commissions from subscriptions to scenes linked from my website. Sometimes the producer I work for has a great cinematic vision, but not a lot of money. They're often a performer themselves. We share the rights to the movie and I hope to make up the income in sales. When the easiest way to find that video is on a tube site, neither I nor the director I loved working for will get paid. I regularly come across a video I was in that has been viewed over 200,000 times. If even a fraction of those views had been paid for, the company could raise performer pay, and increase the quality and frequency of its work.

I advocate for increased performer rights and more visions of adult film in one of the most vilified professions on the planet. I've seen the beauty of erotic cinema and know there's still untapped potential. We're turned away from grants, and shunned by viewers who scoff at the idea of paying for porn. Instead of soaring to new creative heights and showing the magnificent possibilities of human desire, studios can barely survive on shoestring budgets. We're working in the most underpaid film genre. (Some days, working in porn feels a lot like my days in arts administration, minus the State funding.)

Imagine an independent adult filmmaker being able to pay top prices, to cover STI tests, wardrobe, and travel expenses, to produce high-quality content, and to put forth the kinds of amazing images that push forward the representations of human sexuality.

So, what can we do to advance the industry?

1. **Pay for your porn.** This is the best and most direct way to encourage the work you love. If you don't know where to start, take to social media and start following performers. They'll share the work from companies they've enjoyed working for. Many create custom videos, too. Become a porn patron.

2. **Help others find porn you like (or that they might like).** If you're in a position to blog or share posts about porn, you can help others find companies to watch. If you're a sex blogger, journalist, or sex educator, you're also in a unique position to educate your readers and students about how paying for porn can shape the kinds of sexual representation available for all to enjoy. (Plus, use that link

love to earn affiliate commissions from your recommen-dations. It's a win–win.)

3. **Keep enjoying porn.** If you're going to watch porn for free and you're finding videos you like and you aren't convinced that you need to change, then there's not much I can do to stop you. Go forth, but please keep in mind where the work comes from. Allow me to plant a seed, a promise that you'll support us in a more direct way when-ever you can.

We can still make right of the issue. Ethical viewers have incredible potential to shape the industry by "voting with their wallets" and encouraging producers' interests, in everything from distribution methods to casting decisions. Increasing production quality, broadening diversity, build-ing sustainable businesses. Remember there's more to porn than the blazing tube site in the sky that is PornHub—seek it out and encourage its creation, whether through supportive words, network, or wallet.

My motto in porn has been "Be the porn you want to see in the world." But in this case, a better fit is "BUY the porn you want to see in the world." Let's enjoy sexuality, consensually.

The original version of this piece was published on www.jizlee.com.

There's No Rulebook for This

TOBI HILL-MEYER

"Don't hug people; there's no reason to hug people in the workplace." I was working at my campus LGBTQ student group, and the school had arranged for all student groups to get training on sexual harassment. My "workplace" lacked a lot of formalities you might expect from most. Each of us was paid just $100 per month, and while I technically had a boss, it wasn't like most work environments, and you wouldn't keep doing it unless you cared about the people you worked with.

The trainer suggested handshakes instead of hugs. "Or maybe a gentle hand on the shoulder—but that's the extent of physical contact in the workplace that is appropriate."

Her expertise, it turned out, was as a sexual harassment defense lawyer. She didn't seem to care about the ethics of equal opportunity in the workplace, nor did she see sexual harassment as a problem that needed to be addressed. Her main concern seemed to be helping people avoid getting sued. She shared several stories of her clients—all of whom were managers who made innocent comments or inauspicious touches that got misinterpreted.

She told us about one client who had merely complimented an employee's jacket and got sued for it—at least that was his side of the story—and she therefore implored us to avoid ever commenting on someone else's appearance. Ultimately, it was clear that she prioritized the prevention of lawsuits over the prevention of harassment and discrimination. When I asked her to comment on non-discrimination law and how to avoid transphobia in the workplace, she said, "Oh, there's no statewide law on discrimination against trans people, so be sure to look up your local laws, because it varies by city." Then she added, "And never, ever, ask a coworker about their sexual orientation."

Clearly none of this was going to work for our LGBTQ center. The training was near useless. But once you took a moment to separate out the "suggestions" the trainer made from the "rules" the university had, it was easy enough to follow. And while some areas were arguable, there were certain basics that seemed almost universal. Things like professors shouldn't hit on their students and managers shouldn't hit on their employees. Don't hire or fire based on someone's attractiveness or willingness to have sex with you. In fact, it's probably best just to have a sex-free workplace.

It wasn't long after that, however, that I found myself in a new field. I was working in the porn industry. And just like professional corporate prohibitions on hugging didn't make sense in my student union, suddenly those basics that I had thought were universal didn't quite make sense anymore.

When my job became literally to have sex with someone, and cast parties and award shows often become orgies, practically every rule I had known about workplace etiquette and sex was thrown out the window. But that doesn't mean sexual harassment and violations of consent are impossible in the porn industry. It's still very important to create a safe work environment. So in an industry where attractiveness is a bona fide workplace requirement and having sex with or in front of your coworkers and your boss is the job requirement, what rules about workplace sexual harassment are you supposed to follow?

Some producers handle the situation by drawing a strict boundary that they will never personally have sex with the talent. This can work well in traditional porn businesses. Deciding who gets cast is a huge power, and returning to the whole "Don't have sex with employees you supervise" rule, this makes a lot of sense.

However, a lot of porn doesn't look like the old model anymore. Very few performers can make a living wage just by being cast in other people's porn films. You've got to set up your own website. Release your own content. You might do a content trade, where neither you nor your costar gets paid, but you both own the rights to the footage, which you both sell through your websites. In that kind of situation, there is no employer—or perhaps you could say that we all become employers, and everyone is hiring each other.

This dynamic is exacerbated within feminist-driven queer porn, if for no other reason than it is a very small community. And it was even smaller when I started out about a decade ago. When I produced my first film, I was mostly hiring my friends, my partners, my friends' partners, and my partners' friends. In fact, while I was still trying to figure out my performance style, I felt most comfortable only performing with an existing partner. As the producer who was hiring all of the cast, this created an odd prerequisite that you had to be romantically or sexually involved with me to get hired for any scene that I was in.

As soon as I had enough funding and casting resources that I didn't need to perform in my own films, I stopped. It just seemed easier to keep performing and producing separate. Whether I was working for someone else or producing a scene with performers I wasn't personally involved with, it just seemed like there was less opportunity for me to create any inappropriate situations. It worked for a while, but it was a luxury I ultimately couldn't afford. When funding got tight, content trades or performing in my own scenes were the best ways to cut costs.

Sometimes I wondered if I was overthinking all of this. When I'm giving someone a couple hundred dollars for a half day of work, should that forever alter our relationship to employer and employee? Would I really be worrying about this to such a degree if I were hiring friends and lovers to mow my lawn or help me out with housecleaning? Should I?

With the economy the way it is for my generation, more and more people are turning to entrepreneurship to find ways to squeak out just enough money to survive on. Whether it's putting up a donation button or patron campaign for your blog or podcast, selling crafts on Etsy, working as a cam girl, or producing spoken-word shows, a lot of us have worked outside the typical W-2 employment.

If you ask your friend you've got a crush on to draw up an image to go with your podcast and you decide to give them $50 because you're making money off your podcast, does that make them your employee and off-limits? What if a friend of a friend needs help filling the holiday rush of orders for their Etsy store and they pay you for a few hours of working a hot glue gun? Is it okay to ask them out to drinks afterward? And what happens if it turns into more than drinks?

Some people would be tempted to point to how their situation is different and none of the rules apply to them, but of course it's not like all bets are off. If you get a TaskRabbit job cleaning a stranger's house and halfway through the job they decide they've fallen in love with you and won't take the hint that you're not interested, it's obviously not okay.

For quite a while I struggled with the lack of existing guidelines, just taking each decision one at a time and following my personal sense of ethics. Difficult situations certainly came up. The truth is that we all prefer to work with those that we admire. Mix that with the tendency to see sex more lightheartedly when it is a regular part of your work, and situations will come up.

Many of the people who wanted to perform in my films were also fans of my porn performances. Sometimes a performer would even flirt with me on set. I may have even otherwise been receptive, but I would become very awkward with the fear of mishandling the situation. In a way that I found surprising but probably seems obvious from the outside, it made me quite uncomfortable. Eventually, I realized that I was so concerned with making sure that everything was okay for anyone I hired that I never stopped to think about the possibility that I—even as the boss in this scenario—might be the one who was made uncomfortable by being hit on in the workplace.

It helped me to realize that I could create rules for my own productions based not on corporate policies or sexual harassment laws, but on my own interpretation of what would have the best impact on supporting the spirit behind them. The standard performer paperwork that I'd send out in advance of a shoot included a policy not to flirt or make advances toward anyone on set except your scene partner. Clear guidelines helped a lot. If you wanted to hit on someone you met on set—me included—then just wait until it was all done and everyone had been paid.

I also included a rule that performers must not be visibly intoxicated, because even if they insisted to me that they were consenting and comfortable with having sex while intoxicated, I'm the one who would ultimately be responsible if something went wrong. The guidelines became a living document that could have additions or adjustments as I began to anticipate more situations and get feedback from performers and other producers. I kept the rules as basic as possible, and tried to create space for that feedback and conversation when there was a circumstance that anyone felt uncomfortable with.

It's not perfect and I certainly don't claim to have all the answers in this complicated, interwoven set of roles and responsibilities, but if there is one thing I learned it's that you have to adapt to the situation. I couldn't give a strict set of rules that would work across the gig economy, because what makes sense for hiring someone to help you with a project won't necessarily work when you're bringing on a partner to collaborate. And it makes a difference if you found someone from an ad on Craigslist, if you know them through community, if they are an ex, or if they are your friend with benefits. Not to mention that the specific dynamic you have with someone can make a huge difference. Working with an ex you're on good terms with is a world of difference from the ex you just got dumped by and are still sore from.

At one point, I even sought advice from a lawyer, just to make sure things were on the up and up, and he shared with me a perspective that opened up my world. People make a huge deal about sexual relationships, but any relationship can be a problem. Hiring someone you are really close with has the potential to create any number of workplace conflicts. People may see you as giving them preferential treatment. It can cause major fallout if you ever have to fire them. And that's true whether you have a sexual relationship with them, or they are a really close platonic friend, or they are a family member.

Don't assume that a sex-free workplace is a drama-free workplace, and don't assume that mixing sexual relationships with work relationships is an automatic recipe for disaster. What's more important is that everyone involved is able to navigate these complex social interactions, that employers are prepared to take responsibility for problems in the workplace, that employees are ready to communicate when they're having a problem, and that you're confident in everyone's ability to work through issues when they arise.

Admittedly, having a workplace where all of that falls into place is a very tall order. That's why larger institutions have to set up strict rules. Because when I think of the W-2 of most workplaces I've been in, I wouldn't trust all my coworkers to meet that standard. Companies with a few hundred employees won't have that communication and relationship management skill set. Not to mention the high likelihood that some of those employees are outright jerks.

When you bring things down to the level of going into business with your friend of ten years and together hiring their partner, however, maybe you do know everyone involved well enough to make that call. It won't guarantee that problems won't come up; in fact, they probably still will, but the question is how likely you believe it is that you will be able to avoid the worst of them and how prepared you are to deal with the ones you can't avoid. That's just as true if you're making a porn film or offering duos as an escort as it is if you're directing a performance showcase or starting a cleaning service.

Service with a Smile Is Not Consent

CAMERYN MOORE

I recently received a friend request on Facebook, and followed up by asking the person how they found me—my standard operating procedure to avoid phishing, fakes, and "fat-girl collectors" (fat fetishists who are just looking for free photos to wank to). This friend-seeker said, "I found you from a picture on Instagram; a friend of mine does a poet-for-hire busking thing in London. I saw you and thought you looked hot." (This was presumably a picture of me doing Sidewalk Smut, where I set up my manual typewriter on a busy sidewalk and type up custom erotica on commission.)

Normally I would delete and ignore. It's my response of choice for people (almost entirely guys) who lead with come-ons on social media. But I am trying to cultivate potential audiences in the United Kingdom, and this was a relatively mild offense. So, in a moment of weakness, I told the person I would accept their friend request, but was putting them on notice for being inappropriate with me, that I had a one-strike-you're-out policy for out-of-place come-ons. Their response?

"But you kind of operate in literal erotica that's going to arouse readers."

My "literal erotica" arouses readers; therefore, I must be available for flirting, when that is not the service I advertise? My job involves writing things that excite people; therefore, I should be personally available to anyone who is excited by anything I do or say or am?

Some jobs seem like obvious targets for this kind of treatment, but in fact, working women can be and are sexualized, whatever the actual workplace. There is a whole genre of Halloween costumes dedicated to the sexualization of women at work; sexy construction worker, sexy doctor, sexy teacher, sexy lawyer. I would argue that this is almost a corollary of Rule 34 ("If it exists, there is porn of it"): If it's a job, someone has tried to sex it up for women. These jobs are not inherently sexualized jobs—i.e., you don't need secondary sex characteristics to do them, nor do they involve the performance of sex/sexuality/sex wisdom—but that doesn't matter. Male entitlement goes in and stakes a claim wherever the fuck it wants.

I'm focusing, right now, on the jobs that specifically entail dressing up sexy, talking about sex (whether being sexy or not), moving sexily, having real or simulated sex on camera, or having real sex in person. In short, jobs that involve sex or the performance of sexiness.

We may really enjoy those jobs, for different reasons, or maybe we're doing them just to make money. Usually it's some combination thereof, but here's the thing:

They're just work.

These jobs have specifically defined parameters, or we have our own hard-won standards for the work that we do: $250/hour for a sexual encounter, $25 per person at a dirty-talk workshop, $100 plus royalties for erotica, $14 per ticket for a solo play (for seven shows). My street marketing necessarily involves a lot of friendliness and cleavage.

However, our doing the work does not constitute consent for anything else that the client or consumer, actual or potential, may want to do outside of my parameters of time and scope of labor. The fact that I have so many sexually charged jobs and gigs, and keep up that attitude on my public profile, doesn't say anything about my general availability or interest in doing with you, after hours, the things that I may do or talk about while I'm working.

The connection between sexual experience and consent is plenty blurred already, particularly with regard to women. If you do or have done something with someone else, or you regularly do this thing with other people, you therefore must be up for this thing with anyone who wants it from you, and any expression about NOT doing that thing is therefore a lie ("She doesn't mean it") or malevolent denial ("That bitch!"). You can see this with disturbing regularity during cop interviews and cross-examining of rape survivors, but we don't even need to go that far: slut-shaming occurs on a spectrum, and the expectations of entitlement are right there in the middle of it. Look at what happens when a sharp-dressed woman doesn't smile at a "complimentary" catcaller: one minute her putative husband is a lucky man, and the next she's a fat bitch whom the catcaller didn't want, anyway.

It's even worse for those of us who "perform" sex or sexuality, or at least harder to get away from. The more skilled and apparently thrilled we are about doing our work, the more people believe that we mean it, we love it. Whatever it is that we do as part of our work hustle and actual work, they mistake the performance of it, for pay or tips, as the actual thing. This is why people often ask me if I get off during phone sex (no).

So, if we do this sexualized work, that implies that we would do the same acts, and should be up for doing them, even if we weren't being paid for them. Accountants and car mechanics get hit up for freebies outside of work; when it comes to sex(ualized) work, "civilians" just go to their own experience of sex, that it's so fun and awesome, why wouldn't we JUMP at the chance to do more of it? I mean, look how enthusiastic and open-minded we are about sex out in public!

Spoiler alert: This is called *performing*. Our job is to make people believe it, when we say, "Ooh yes, right there, I love it," when we take our clothes off and wink at the crowd, when we bend over a little lower to sling the drinks, when we get all sweaty and radiant telling our sex stories to a crowded theater audience, when we talk about our favorite vibrators or even demo them in a private experiential workshop. Being able to convey enthusiasm is a job requirement; our customers and clients and audience members demand it from us, and buy into it, literally. What they don't understand, or often simply choose to ignore, is that our performative enjoyment shuts off when the performance is done. They don't think about it; they just get frustrated and angry when they can't access that same enthusiasm and enjoyment "off the clock."

I am very interested in sex; I happen to believe that we can access a lot of the human condition through discussion about sexuality. I definitely think people need to have more of these authentic conversations about sex, and it is my honor and pleasure to be involved in facilitating some of those conversations. Hell, I have written extensively about my own sexual experiences, and will continue to do so when it forwards the work that I want to do.

But there's that word again: work. What I am doing for pay is still work. It may or may not reflect things I actually want to do in my personal life, and it certainly isn't some sort of oblique come-on to anyone in my range of market saturation. It's my job. And my agreement to do it, in the moment, my passion, my pursuit, even, of those performative moments, does not constitute consent to ANYTHING else.

So you're reading this and thinking, okay, no moves on people on the job, whether it's a "sexy" job or not, no moves without their consent. How do I even interact with them?

First of all, don't buy into the false dichotomy that if you can't hit on someone, you can't talk with them at all. You totally can be friendly and interested.

- Acknowledge that the person is at work, and give them space to interact with other customers and audience members. If it's just too busy, either try back at a less busy time or skip it.
- Whatever job we're doing, ask us good questions that demonstrate you respect our intelligence in the field we're in.
- Compliment us on the performance you just witnessed, with an emphasis on the non-physical feature attributes (e.g., if it's a burlesque show, say "I really liked the way you worked with your props" instead of "UR TITZ R SO BYOOOTIFUL OMG").

AND FINALLY, just don't hit on us. What's true in non-sexy jobs is true in sexy jobs: there's a power dynamic at play. The customer holds all the power and the worker knows it. Even asking for consent takes on a heavier weight when the worker feels as though their income or audience might suffer if they reject such advances. If I'm tending my merch booth after a show, it is not that easy for me to rebuff someone's come-on, because there is an audience all around me, and I also want to sell merch, right?

If you must make a move, wait until the person isn't busy, ask in your best inviting and non-coercive way (to flirt, to kiss, to touch, whatever), and if they say yes, cool. If no, ALSO

COOL. You accept the boundaries that they set. We are talking about people at work, which makes things more complicated for us, the workers.

It is best in these situations is to let us decide. If we want to leave our "sexy" switch on when we are off the clock, if we have the energy for it, that is up to us.

IN THE HOME

Consent Culture Begins at Home

EVE RICKERT AND FRANKLIN VEAUX

There's a saying: charity begins at home.

Every one of us was born into a society that, in one way or another, does not respect our consent or our agency. In nearly every human society, an all-pervasive, fundamental coerciveness is so ubiquitous that it becomes part of the social ocean in which we swim, so much a part of the background that it can be difficult even to see.

This, too, begins at home.

Many people like to say that family is the backbone of society. It's probably more true that families are the seeds from which we as social creatures bloom. But what does family mean? The idea of "family" is preloaded with so much cultural baggage it can be extraordinarily difficult to unpack. We struggled with writing this essay, because trying to apply the notion of consent culture—which, make no mistake, is a radical idea—to family structures quickly creates a knot that no sword can cut.

Families are complex, contradictory beasts. They are built, at the most basic level, from non-consensual relationships. We don't get to choose our family of origin. Indeed, we don't choose to be born at all. Most of us have at least one relative that, given the choice, we'd really rather not be related to.

So, given the inherently non-consensual nature of family, it's probably not surprising that families are paradoxical things that don't yield easily to consent-culture analysis. That fundamentally non-consensual foundation is both blessing and curse, as it turns out.

First, the bad bits.

Most of us pick up terrible ideas about consent and agency from our families of origin. These lessons start early and are reinforced often. Abusive families are obviously built on coercive foundations, but we're not only talking about abusive families when we say this. Coercion plays out in thousands of ways even in families that aren't abusive. The best-known example among consent activists is the mandatory hug: telling a child "You have to give Aunt Mabel a hug!" is coercive, especially from the perspective of a child to whom Aunt Mabel might be a mysterious stranger. We assume that bonds of family and love are transitive—if I love my sister, my child has to as well—but that's not true at all. In fact, it's inherently coercive to expect that one person should offer intimacy to another simply because you do.

That coercion is expressed in more subtle ways as well. Relatives who revel in "embarrassing" us often do so by revealing our most vulnerable stories to people we'd prefer not hear them. If a family member is sick or stressed or dealing with loss, there's often an expectation—often tacit, sometimes explicit—that we must be available to perform emotional or physical labor, or provide material support, for them…even if that person hasn't treated us well. Nearly all of us have had the experience of being expected to get along with people we have little love for, and for some of us, people we've been mistreated by, at family gatherings. (In fact, holidays are often emotional minefields for families.) Many kinds of boundaries, small and large, physical and emotional, are often frowned upon in families.

Those of us in non-traditional chosen families must be wary of becoming too smug, because even in intentional families, coercion and non-consent often form the backdrop of many of our assumptions. Family, no matter how it's defined, is fertile breeding ground for non-consent.

Both of us are polyamorous, and we've seen firsthand how coercion and non-consent play out in polyamorous intentional families. This can be overt, as in couples who insist that a person who wants to be emotionally or sexually intimate with one of them must be emotionally and sexually available to both of them, or be expelled abruptly from the family. Most of us will go to great lengths to preserve our intimate relationships. So if you create an environment where access to a person you love requires that you have sex with or offer emotional intimacy to someone you don't want to be intimate with, that creates an incredibly coercive environment.

Coercion in polyamorous families may also be more subtle, as in polyamorous groups that apply pressure to the folks involved to be close, to not want too much, to share a bed even when they prefer to sleep alone, or to not assert other physical or emotional boundaries.

And abuse in non-traditional chosen families can take on whole new, horrifying dimensions. Gaslighting—the practice of undermining someone's memory or subjective experiences ("You're remembering it wrong," "You don't really feel that way")—can become all the more powerful, and all the more toxic, when multiple people work together to undermine the abuse survivor's perception of reality. (This happens in traditional families too, as when a family works together to silence someone who has been sexually abused by another family member.)

No matter how you slice it, no matter what form the family takes, families are gardens whose soil is thickly sown with the seeds of coercion and uniquely suitable for their germination and growth.

Does that mean, then, we should strive to build families entirely free of coercion? Should we tear down the entire notion of "family" and start over from the ashes?

These are complicated questions. On the one hand, it would seem that coercion is incompatible with a culture of consent. If we are to create cultures of consent, we have to start with our families, both biological and chosen.

On the other hand, the intrinsic non-consensual nature of family is, as weird as this might sound in a book on consent, one of its greatest strengths. Home, as Robert Frost said, is that place where, when you have to go there, they have to take you in.

A functional, healthy family, whether blood or chosen, offers us safety and security. At its best, it offers a stable foundation on which all our other intimate relationships can be built. The people in a healthy family are there for each other through thick and thin; they don't simply walk away when things get rough. In the best of circumstances, a secure family is a guarantee of shelter, food, and connection—and it is therefore a privilege, ensuring that those who have access to one can never fall as far as those who do not.

Ah, but the devil is in the details.

The two of us come from white, American, middle-class families, where individualism is highly valued. We recognize that many others, from different backgrounds, have different experiences of family, and so our commentary is not universal. But as we look around at our own families and at the various non-traditional relationship communities we belong to (also largely white, American, and middle class), we've seen a tension between two completely different ideas about family. First, there's the idea that all healthy relationships are voluntary, and in an ethical, consent-based culture, people are free to leave any relationship that isn't working for them for any reason—or for no reason at all. And second, an ideal that people are not disposable. That families are made up of people who commit to being with one another for the long haul, in good times and bad, and these commitments are not to be taken lightly or thrown away trivially.

It might seem then, on the surface, that the non-consensual nature of families is also what allows them to offer the security that makes them so valuable. However, we propose that this notion is based on a flawed approach to family. The difference lies in *love* and *commitment*. A family that is both secure and consensual requires substantial helpings of both.

Some people imagine that if all interactions are consensual, you never do anything you don't want to do. That's wrong. You can absolutely consent to do things that aren't what you would independently choose. If your sibling needs someone to drive them to the doctor, and you'd much rather be snogging your new partner, you can consent to put your hormones on hold and take care of your family. If you'd really rather have your home to yourself, but your grown-up child has been laid off and lost every penny they own to medical bills, you can consent to give up space and privacy in order to offer them a roof over their head. And in fact, you can consent *in advance* to make these sorts of sacrifices and extend care, before such care is ever needed. That's the nature of commitment. That is, for many, the nature of family.

It may seem obvious through these examples, but it's surprising how often it's not. People get very confused over the difference between commitment and consent; it's one of the things we spend the most time talking about in our workshops. There are a couple of things that seem to trip people up: one is the idea of pre-consenting, and the other is the idea of setting boundaries within the context of commitment.

We say in our first book, *More Than Two,* that you cannot pre-consent to intimacy. This is true. Consent always exists in the moment, and it can always be withdrawn at any time. In the context of family, intimacy typically applies to emotional intimacy: How much information do you share? How much vulnerability do you show? How much influence do you give family members over your choices? How much access do you give to what is yours: your space, your clothing, your money, information about your life? Just as in sex, we believe you cannot pre-consent to these forms of intimacy. You can state an intention for them to be ongoing, and work to maintain conditions where they remain possible, but you always have the right to withdraw consent in the future, and in the moment.

However, we feel a lot of people have confused *intimacy* with *care*. And we believe you *can* pre-consent to care. I can promise to drive you to your chemo appointments, even if it inconveniences me, and that does not violate my consent. If I promise you I will never let you be without shelter as long as I can prevent it, that is a promise I can make and keep, and it does not violate my consent, and never has to—no matter how inconvenienced I may be if and when I have to make good on my promise.

And I can make a promise that acts as a loving container for these other kinds of promises: that we are family, that I will listen to you, that I will make your happiness as important as mine, that I will continue to support and nurture you in whatever ways are available to me when you need that support and nurture.

Such a commitment can be freely, consensually entered into, and honored with love.

It is also possible to set boundaries within the context of even such a broad commitment. As a baseline, this means that our right to give, withhold, and withdraw consent to intimacy, physical or emotional, remains, no matter what kind of other commitments we've made. But as well, we are never required to accept mistreatment. Saying "I will always be there for you" is not blanket permission for another to trample our feelings and needs. Commitment to material and emotional support does not require us to be enablers to destructive or toxic behavior.

Building families on a foundation of consent, then, requires that we understand the distinction between commitment and coercion, and know the difference between guaranteeing someone future intimate access to ourselves and promising to work together to support one another and make a relationship function.

We've talked to people who believe that asking your partner to change their behavior in any way for any reason is inherently controlling. We do not believe this. Asking for what you need in any relationship is both necessary and fundamental to having your needs met; the difference between asking for something and controlling another person lies in whether you are willing to accept no for an answer.

You can't promise intimacy. People change. That doesn't mean you can't offer commitment, only that the commitments you make must be flexible, be freely entered into, and leave room for you to assert boundaries around access to yourself and treatment you will accept.

We propose that families built on consent start from the premise that human beings attach to one another—and when we attach, we then *want* to make choices that support the relationship and the people in it.

After all, isn't that the whole point? We build families not to get what we need, but to work together to reach further, accomplish more, love more, and become more than we can on our own.

Bodily Autonomy for Kids

AKILAH S. RICHARDS

I often hear people talk about pregnancy from a space of gratitude—and sometimes excitement.

Though I agree that the journey is incredible and enriching, there is another, perhaps less embraced aspect. For me, pregnancy was also full of moments of intense vulnerability, fear, and at times, anger. I felt fearful about my own safety, it being so inextricably linked with the safety of the person growing in my belly.

Inadvertent pushes from someone who stood in a line behind me, an overly ambitious driver who darted across my path at an intersection, a woman who threatened me because she (wrongly) assumed I stole her parking spot—all those instances of intense vulnerability and primal fear, stemming from my need to protect my future child.

Even more unnerving were the instances where physical contact with my belly wasn't just implied, *it was accomplished*. This is where my anger would rise to the surface—I'd get angry at the people who felt completely within their rights to touch my belly, to touch my baby. Whether an elderly man or a woman who was also a mother, I resented them for feeling okay with touching my child without permission, even when she was in utero.

For sure, I felt uncomfortable with them trying to touch *my* body—and all that that says about being a woman in a public space. But more than that, it clued me in to many adults' idea that they don't need children's permission to touch them—or to require that they touch someone else.

Today, my daughters are twelve and ten, and I still feel the need to protect them physically—and to advocate for their right to govern their own bodies. But I have to do more than advocate for them.

In a world that constantly sends messages to women about connecting their value with their physicality and desirability, I need to help them operate with an awareness of their right to reject or accept physical touch, or any act that affects their personal space or feeling of safety, from any adult or child.

And that means I have to be honest about the ways that I, myself, might infringe on their personal boundaries, and I have to facilitate these conversations with the adults around me. And I don't just mean conversations about what we can do to protect children, but also about what we must do to *help* children understand their options for protecting their physical and emotional selves.

One way we can approach this goal is to explore some of the common mistakes we adults make when it comes to helping children practice bodily autonomy, which is at the root of consent culture for children. Otherwise, we will continue to do the things that compromise the self-confidence, the sense of safety and bodily autonomy, and the mental wellness of the children we love. Because the reality is that children are coerced into situations where their bodies are treated as the property of their parents.

These instances vary from making them hug a family member to trading their body for sex, drugs, or even food. All of these instances can send a message to children that their bodies are not their own. They also blur the lines between safe and unsafe touch, and consent versus coercion, and make it difficult for many children to identify when they're being inappropriately or uncomfortably touched by an adult or another child.

Many of us send messages that lessen their ability to recognize and trust what feels safe and uncomfortable for them, as well as how to confidently communicate with an adult they trust when their personal boundaries are violated by anyone, including an adult or child they know and trust.

Statistically, the percentages are wildly unnerving: 90% of child sexual abuse victims know the perpetrator in some way, and 68% are abused by family members. What's more staggering is that 90% are abused by someone they know, love, or trust, and that 20% of child sexual abuse victims are under the age of eight. Most of them don't tell until they become adults. One of the reasons for this is that as children, they don't have language around those feelings. No one is talking to them about their right to feel safe in their own bodies—to have and assert personal boundaries as a way of protecting themselves.

Consent culture is often confined to the topic of consensual sex or intimacy among adults, but it should extend toward all behaviors and to children. Similarly, the term *bodily autonomy* tends to be more widely recognized under a specific topic: reproductive justice advocacy—and more specifically, the pro-choice movement for abortion rights.

So as to extend these important concepts beyond the scope of sex and reproduction, let's look how parents' mistakes around bodily autonomy can contradict the practice of consent culture among children. Because when children don't feel sure about inappropriate touch, we must look at the narratives around body ownership and consent. For this reason, we must look at confident body autonomy for all people, even before they become adults, and outside of the context of sex.

I believe one of the biggest mistakes we make as parents is in teaching children to ignore their personal boundaries. In the United States, we have a subtle history of showing children that their bodies are owned by their parents. Forced physical contact with relatives reinforces the dangerously wrong message that relatives can't be abusers. *"Grandpa just wants to hug you—don't back away,"* or other similar verbal prompts, tells children to ignore their feelings about a person (whether based on intuition or past experience) and listen to what an adult says instead.

As well-meaning observers, we adults often infringe on personal boundaries within children's interactions. Coercing a reserved child to hold hands and dance around with an outgoing child may feel like we're helping that child develop good social skills. But what we may actually do is teach them that it's okay for other people to force them to do what makes other people comfortable.

In later years, that can cause some children to feel that they need to be forced to do things, or that their natural tendency is somehow not okay. This can also have long-term negative effects on their social skills, because self-esteem and authentic friendships are difficult to form and maintain when a person isn't okay with who and how they innately are.

Also, many children who endure sexual abuse in particular don't tell because they're afraid of being blamed for being complicit in the abuse. This tells us that children don't understand abuse. That's in part because we, the adults, don't give them the language to name these experiences, and to feel safe coming to us about them.

Difficult aspects of personal boundary violation, particularly peer-to-peer abuse, make it extra-complicated for adults to feel clear on how to broach the topic with children. But children need to know that other children can be abusers and that they can abuse another child by touching them without permission, even if that child has told them *yes* in the past.

Whether subtle or overt, the effects of childhood body violations are that we don't feel that we own ourselves. I know this from personal experience. We feel uncomfortable, unsure, or even afraid about asserting dominion over our own bodies. And again, it's important to realize that our bodies and our boundaries exist outside of sex, and that consent is required for anything having to do with our bodies.

A solution to the blurred lines of personal boundaries is to practice parenting without coercion. Consent culture should start with children, and when children grow up believing that all people have the right to control and protect their own bodies, they're likely to respect other people's boundaries and to speak up when boundaries—whether their own or those of others—are being violated.

§

Another place parents may stumble is instead of starting positive, developmentally appropriate conversation about bodies, sex, and intimacy in general, they tend to omit those terms when conversing with their children. I believe it's a mistake to do so, and it reinforces shame or silence around body-related feelings. Getting comfortable with saying *penis, vagina, anus,* or even the more popular (and maybe less easy to hear from a child) slang terms like *butthole,* for example, can lessen the feeling of shame around talking about private body parts or body-related feelings.

These same types of conversations can also help children feel equipped to communicate with someone they trust if they are being sexually violated, for example. This way, we're not just giving them language about what's happening with them, we're also helping them express what's happening *to* them. If they're comfortable naming them, then they have language to use when those body parts are affected by anyone in any way.

Another word that often goes unspoken among parents to children in healthy ways is *masturbation*. It's normal for children's curiosity to include their own bodies, sometimes showing up as self-pleasuring. Labeling that form of self-exploration as *bad*, or avoiding the topic with your child altogether, can make it difficult for a child to feel comfortable with their own body and physical feelings. As caring adults, one way we can nurture safe spaces for children is to educate ourselves on taboo topics like masturbation and children, particularly prepubescent children.

Some of us may have incorrect ideas about masturbation based on our parents' perspectives or other aspects of our own introduction to sexuality. But our children are not us, and though they are our responsibility, their bodies and experiences are their own. In support of this, we can read, discuss, and watch our way toward a sex-positive approach to parenting so that our children feel safe asking questions and know that they can discuss any aspect of their bodies with us, including sensations and thoughts that they may find pleasurable.

Personally, I address masturbation with my daughters in part because I don't ever want to set the precedent that anyone (even their mother) needs to validate how to explore aspects of their sexuality. My intention is to avoid making masturbation an issue of morality or appropriateness, and instead focus on what is socially safe and personally hygienic. In other words, as Lea Grover so perfectly stated in her piece This Is What Sex-Positive Parenting Really Looks Like, "We don't play with our vulvas at the table."

The last mistake I want to talk about is neglecting to teach your child the importance of their intuition. Intuition is not exclusive to adulthood, and it can play a very important role in helping a child develop a healthy sense of bodily autonomy. At any age, we have feelings in our bellies or chests, for example, that are directly triggered by feelings of safety or lack thereof. Help children to name and acknowledge those feelings—and to trust them.

One way I practice nurturing intuition is to help children understand what intuition does. For my girls, I like the simple definition of intuition as a kind of internal safety alarm. I give them specific examples of times that I listened to my intuition and kept myself safe, and times that I ignored my intuition and wasn't sure how to protect myself when I faced danger. I'm not always sure if this is effective, but it helps me be sure that I'm practicing what I believe will work and what has worked with them in prior instances. Asking them how intuition feels for them is good, too. That way, they've verbalized the feelings and can more easily recognize and even share them when they show up.

Some parents tend to direct their child on how they should interact with a new adult, instead of watching and seeing how their child responds to them and going from there. That's an example of intuitive interference. In order for a child to develop a sense of trust in their own intuition, we as parents have to respect their choices, and decide on a safe place and time to discuss the interaction and see if our child has questions. This is where we parents can be advocates and allies for our children.

For example, if I meet up with a friend who has an outgoing child and I have my bona fide introvert in tow, I tell that parent that my daughter may or may not play with their child. Or that she may not hug them, or participate in any well-meaning small talk. I often bring books, games, and even art supplies along so that my daughter can feel comfortable when she's accompanying me somewhere, without feeling pushed to engage with anyone, child or adult, unless she chooses to do so.

We can also tell our children about our own experiences with intuition and encourage them to talk, write about, or act out moments when they recognized intuitive feelings. When we parent without addressing intuitive feelings and how to express them, we can miss opportunities to convey the importance of words like "no" and "stop," or phrases like "I don't want to" or "I don't like that."

If a child is playing with someone whose body language or verbal cues lead the child to start feeling uncomfortable, we can tell them that an uneasy feeling in their belly or chest is enough to warrant their saying "no," "stop," or "I don't like that," because their body is their own, and they get to choose what is done to it. And, more than that, they get to express their choice through consent or refusal.

Also tell them that it's important that they stop whatever they're doing to someone else's body when that person uses those key terms. This way, we help children to start exploring the reality that they may not agree with or understand why someone is saying "no" to them, and that the person does not need to explain whatever they're declining. Saying "no" is enough.

§

There are examples among children in all parts of the world that stem from lack of consent where children are concerned. Certainly, this includes sexual abuse, as is the normal conversation around consent culture, but it includes more. It also includes non-sexual activities and daily occurrences that offer opportunities to practice consent culture in all aspects of living.

The point here is to become much more proactive about preventing sexual and other forms of physical abuse by adults to children, and among children as well. We may not be able to prevent all instances, but if we raise young people who are clear about personal boundaries and armed with language and clarity about their feelings and bodily rights, we can minimize these instances as well as the harm done by them. And we can stop the cycle of children who become adults wrestling with unresolved pain and trauma from their bodies not being treated as their own property.

This piece was originally published at everydayfeminism.com.

To Keep a Roof Over My Head, I Consented to Delaying My Transition

LAURA KATE DALE

When I hit puberty in my late teens, I worked out pretty quickly that I was uncomfortable in my body and needed to do something about that. Designated male at birth, the onset of prominent Adam's apple growth, facial hair growth, vocal deepening, and frequent erections suddenly instilled in me a deep-seated discomfort I couldn't shake.

Every minute. Every day. I was uncomfortable in my own skin.

The sudden onset of dysphoric feelings toward my body soon led me to discover the concept of gender transition, the revelation that there was a way for me to hopefully make myself feel more at home in my own body. I messed around with clothing, voice, and name usage privately at home, away from the world, and the results of early experimentation with presentation were reassuring. I could see a future for myself I had not been able to see in a long time.

As I was still living with my parents, progressing with transition while under their roof was going to be tough without them finding out. I decided to bite the bullet and just tell my mother up front what I was experiencing, what I intended to do about it, and offer to answer any questions. She quietly

listened to what I had to say, told me not to rush into anything, and said nothing more of it. I later learned she felt a
sense of mourning akin to the death of a child.

I told my stepfather about my feelings of dysphoria angrily
in a fight at the dinner table. He claimed I was playing up my
recently onset depression as a way to avoid taking responsibility for my future. I angrily told him how I felt about my
body, how large a factor it was in my depression, and that I
intended to transition as soon as I was able.

I was kicked out the house by my stepfather that night. I
was given ten minutes to pack up my things and get out.

The reasons he gave? He wasn't ready to deal with me.
He wasn't ready to deal with friends and family knowing. He
wasn't ready to be judged by those around him. He wasn't
ready to lose a son, even one as lacking in traditional masculinity as I was. In his defense, he was in his mid-sixties. He
is undoubtedly a product of an era where LGBT acceptance
was a rarity.

I was a homeless queer teenager for roughly six weeks. Of
that time I spent maybe ten days sofa surfing with friends, not
telling them that I was homeless but taking advantage of the
chance to get myself clean, warm, fed, and dry. I told some
friends that our hot water had broken. I told others we had a
power cut. I'm fairly sure at least a couple of them knew. I was
certainly not in any place to begin transition; I was far more
concerned with getting through one day after another.

The six weeks I spent homeless were terrifying. I isolated
myself from others out of a nebulous fear of being taken
advantage of in any way. I slept behind beach huts where I
had access to outdoor showers, public bathrooms, and drinking water nearby. I cried myself to sleep most nights. I made
enough money delivering newspapers to survive on. I spent

the rest of each day not really doing anything but sitting, waiting, often crying.

When I was presented an option to come back and live in my parents' house again, I was ready to snap at the offer. A roof over my head. Power and Internet. A bed. Food. Hot showers and baths. I was ready to do anything to go back home.

There was a caveat: I had to put off transition for at least one year.

There was no guarantee that when the year was up I would be permitted to transition under their roof, just that the decision would be readdressed after a year. I would have to wait a year to seek help halting the effects of testosterone-fueled puberty. I would have to accept that my transition would be happening on their terms, based on their level of comfort with the idea over time.

I accepted my parents' offer.

Looking back, I probably should have gone behind my parents' back and started the process of arranging medical help with transition straightaway. The process of getting any kind of medical intervention takes well over a year regardless, and many of the early effects of hormones and blockers can be hidden from the world for a while, but out of fear of being kicked back out onto the street I put transition largely on hold.

I didn't want to take any chances regarding stable housing.

I highly regret my decision to delay transition. I constantly wonder how much of my testosterone puberty could have been prevented from making irreversible changes to my body if I hadn't spent that year waiting. Would my facial hair currently be easier to manage? Would it be less thick and coarse? Would my voice be less deep? Would I have had smaller feet and been able to more easily purchase shoes in my size?

How much difference did that twelve-month delay make to my body?

I consented to wait that year. I consented in a situation where I didn't really have any other choice. As a queer teenager my options were consenting to changes to my body that would be hard to reverse, or continuing to be homeless.

I don't know that consent under those circumstances is really consent.

In the years since things have improved. My parents are now fully supportive of my transition, I've had surgery and am on hormone replacement therapy, and my life is going nowhere but up. My life is in a good place, but my transition will always in part belong to my parents. I can't change the fact that my parents made choices that forever impacted my appearance and quality of life.

I wonder if I made the right choice by agreeing to put my life on hold.

IN THE HOSPITAL

Giving Birth When Black

TAKEALLAH RIVERA

I spent most of my adult life battling physicians for the right to access a long-term birth-control method, only to constantly be denied and told that I was "too young for an IUD" and that "sterilization was not an option because I was too young and would eventually meet a nice man who wanted children."

When I was twenty-three years old, I became pregnant with my first child, after experiencing birth-control failure. At the time, I had recently left an abusive relationship with my child's biological father and was penniless, left homeless after he had left a Greyhound bus ticket on my nightstand because he "could not deal with the situation." I had only a small bag of items to my name. With nowhere to go, I relocated back to my hometown of Memphis, Tennessee, where I settled onto my mom's lumpy couch and began to rebuild my life while simultaneously preparing to take care of a small, helpless child in less than thirty-two weeks.

During this time, I began to search for community resources and completely immersed myself in all things infant- and toddler-related. Throughout the early stages of my pregnancy, I made decisions about where I would give birth and with whom (as a sexual assault survivor, I had my heart set on giving birth with a midwife, whom I would solely see throughout the duration of my pregnancy and postpartum periods), how I would feed my child (breastfeeding for the win!), and what foods I would introduce to my small child. However, every decision I made was met with turmoil. Upon attempting to secure a midwife for my pregnancy, I discovered that no insurance in the state of Tennessee covers midwifery care. "Maybe I could pay for the cost out of pocket!" I thought. Wrong again. At nearly $3,000, there was no way I could possibly afford a midwife as a low-income woman. I cried and raged for days.

Feeling broken and upset, I gave in and began to research local hospitals and choose where I would deliver my child. Because I was on Medicaid, I had only two options of where I would give birth. I began researching the two hospitals that I had to choose between. During my search, I was mind-blown by the local cesarean section rates in my community. After careful research, I decided on giving birth at Baptist Memorial Hospital for Women, which had one of the lowest cesarean section rates in the community: 39.9% (yes, this was one of the lowest in the county—let that sink in).

Throughout my entire pregnancy, labor, and delivery, I noticed that virtually none of my needs, wants, or requests were listened to or respected. The birth plan that I worked on for nine months was tossed to the side once I was admitted into the hospital to induce my labor. As a sexual assault survivor, I was very clear that I did not do too well with multiple people being present during my labor and delivery, nor was I at all comfortable with multiple providers conducting my vaginal exams. Because I was under pain-relieving medication, which altered my abilities, I was especially concerned with strangers conducting my vaginal exams. I remember waking up twice during my laboring process and feeling a stranger's fingers inside my vagina. I remember crying about it, yet not being able to move due to the pain medication I was on. I also requested to not have numerous people present during my delivery—there were five strangers staring at my vulva while I pushed. I felt silenced, ridiculed, and unsafe. I did not get to enjoy my pregnancy, labor, or delivery, because my voice about my own body was not honored.

Fortunately, I gave birth vaginally to a healthy baby boy on April 10, 2013, at 1:03 a.m. I was excited and relieved that my baby had finally arrived. But I was enraged. I was enraged that I was not given a choice of where and how I could deliver the child I had carried for over nine months. "I wonder how many other Black women feel this way?" I thought to myself. When my son was barely a month old, I began to train as a doula and dig deeper into the history of doulas and midwives in the United States. What I discovered pissed me off to the point of tears, and I have been pissed off ever since. The United States has a dark history of pushing out Black doulas and midwives who helped deliver healthy Black babies with zero-mortality rates. Babies born by the hands of Black doulas and midwives were strong and healthy, and their mothers were well nurtured and cared for throughout their pregnancies. This is completely opposite to the treatment that the cold, Eurocentric, Westernized model of medicine had to offer. When these women were pushed out of their professions by racist, sexist Westernized doctors and governing bodies, Black maternal and infant health declined rapidly.

Per a recent study, every forty-eight seconds a Black infant passes away in my hometown, Memphis, Tennessee. This is a city that is over 60% Black. Studies have proven that the African American infant mortality rate is four times higher than the white infant mortality rate. Black women are also more likely to deliver their babies prematurely and have low-weight babies than their white counterparts. Partner this with the fact that only 59% of Black women breastfeed, compared to nearly 75% of white women. Black mothers are cheated out of their autonomy and Black babies are cheated out of their health even before they are born! It has been constantly proven that the Westernized medical model has constantly failed Black women and children, yet, despite these findings, the Westernized medical model is constantly pushed on Black women and our children. We're discouraged from home and water births, we have our family and community members pushed out of our delivery rooms to make room for medical students for "observation," and our needs for successful breastfeeding are oftentimes ignored.

So, what can we do about this?

Many white birth activists' solution for decreasing Black infant mortality and cesarean rates and increasing Black women's breastfeeding rates are to train and place more doulas and midwives in low-income communities. However, this solution is not a solution at all—it is merely the white savior complex wrapped in cultural appropriation and classism. Doula trainings from governing bodies, such as DONA, are ridiculously expensive, which locks out many low-income women and Women of Color from the profession. Also, many white doulas do not market to or cater to lower-income Women of Color (especially with services that range from $800 to $2,500), and many white doulas feel that offering pro bono doula services to low-income Women of Color would be "devaluing" the doula profession. But, the doula profession was devalued long ago when veteran and highly experienced Black doulas and midwives were pushed out of their professions by Eurocentric literacy tests and Westernized medical standards.

From my experiences as a low-income, single Black mother and doula and the research I conducted during my pregnancy, I've concluded that we have had the tools all along to decrease Black maternal and infant mortality rates, to improve Black breastfeeding rates, and to level the playing fields when it comes to all things birth- and baby-related—we simply do not want to use these tools. Placing Black maternal and Black infant health back into the nurturing hands of those who know Black women and Black babies best (Black midwives, doulas, and lactation consultants) would be far too easy and would give Black women the agency and autonomy that has been stripped from us constantly over the years. When I think of the state of Black maternal and infant health, I think of the enslaved Black women who were victims of highly unethical medical experiments conducted by James Marion Sims, who ironically was credited as "the father of modern gynecology." I think of Henrietta Lacks, a poor Black tobacco farmer whose cells were taken without her knowledge and used to make medical strides in vaccines, cloning, and in vitro fertilization. I think of enslaved women who had their babies ripped from their breasts and had their slave master's children forced upon their breasts to feed, while their babies starved to death. I think of Sybrina Fulton, Valerie Bell, Lesley McSpadden, and hundreds of other Black women who gave birth to beautiful Black children despite these circumstances, yet had their babies taken from them due to white supremacy and police brutality. I think of the thousands of Black women who did not (and still do not) have access to adequate prenatal education, health care, or even a choice of where and how they give birth. Black women are owed endless gratitude and compensation for our physical, emotional, and mental labor, and our babies are owed the world—but the only ones fighting for us and our babies are other Black women.

As white and non-Black People of Color, before you reach out to Black women to support your causes, I challenge you to ask yourselves "Did I hire a Black doula for her doula and education services and compensate her for them? Have I offered to support a Black woman on her quest to becoming a doula or midwife? When was the last time I marched for Black women and children? When was the last time I advocated for Black maternal and infant health? When was the last time I put myself on the line the same way that Black women have done for me?"

Fatphobia and Consent: How Social Stigma Mitigates Fat Women's Autonomy

VIRGIE TOVAR

In July of 2016, a model named Dani Mathers, who was the 2015 Playboy Playmate of the Year, was at the center of outrage online. She took an image of an unknowing naked woman who was changing at the gym, and uploaded the image to Snapchat with the caption "If I can't unsee this then you can't either."

The image is a bit hazy, but one could surmise that the woman is over fifty. She is not slender. The joke is that seeing an older fat woman naked is so fundamentally upsetting that Mathers was permanently scarred by the experience ("can't unsee"). That she chose to share it on Snapchat indicates she felt this sentiment was not only acceptable but that her act of invasion would gain traction online from her following.

The woman who was non-consensually photographed had a body type that was closer to mine than to Dani Mathers'. One of my biggest fears as a fat woman is being photographed non-consensually by someone who seeks to violate my privacy and autonomy for sport.

It's happened before.

Once I was on the train, commuting to downtown San Francisco, when a group of teenagers got on. They sat right in front of me on the otherwise empty train, and started taking group selfies. When I looked up I saw one of them showing his friend the zoomed-in image of my face, while he pointed and laughed. It turned out that photographing me was the real reason behind the selfies: just my body *existing* was funny to them. It has since made me hypervigilant while on the train.

Now I consciously avoid two sets of commuter hours, attempting to weave around the 9 to 5 set who are heading to and from work, as well as the high school students who get out of school at 3 p.m. Both of them pose a threat to my sense of safety in public.

Once I was a high school teacher. One of my male colleagues took me aside and told me that a student had texted everyone at the small school a zoomed-in picture of my ass. He showed it to me on his phone. No head, no torso, just my butt. The student had taken the picture while I was writing an assignment on the whiteboard. For the remainder of the year I didn't feel comfortable writing on the board in my own classroom. I was too embarrassed to hold the student accountable.

Some of the coverage on the Dani Mathers event sought to reduce this behavior to "bullying." Referring to this behavior with the infantilizing language of "bullying" seeks to lessen the severity of the behavior and downplay its truly violatory nature. This is no accident: the invocation of "bullying" is part of an apologist lexicon that seeks to downplay and depathologize the violent behavior of those who are enforcing cultural norms. In fact, this is an instance of *sexual assault*.

By exonerating the perpetrator, the violent behaviors and systems that bolster the culture as we know it become normalized. Emotionally violent behavior with lifelong effects is quickly—and wrongfully—glossed over by using this kind of language.

When people systematically target an already stigmatized group, like fat women, their behavior confirms and activates inferiority-based ideologies. These ideologies are enforced often through social mechanisms that seek to ostracize and punish people who are being non-compliant.

In the case of fat women, the culture offers us an unacceptable ultimatum: become thin or disappear. If you do not consent to the terms, you are fair game. The idea that stigmatized groups are "asking for it" when we engage in behaviors deemed inappropriate for our status isn't new.

This idea maps onto the neoliberal notion that is a cornerstone of American life: bootstrapping. Bootstrapping gains traction through the imagined notion of consent; it argues that we are all given an equal chance at success and that if we do not achieve success it is because we did not *desire* success enough. This ideology has strong roots in the current version of U.S. capitalism, but it is not only in the arena of personal finance that we see this ideology manifest.

Bootstrapping is also the basis for dieting. It is through dieting that we indicate to the culture at large that we have consented to fatphobia and are willing to live under the terms of bigotry. When we refuse to consent to that, we are considered hostile and become targets of regulation.

Social media becomes an extension of public life, where we can perform our willingness or unwillingness to play along. Likewise, people often treat social media as an extension of public space, and it is regulated in that way. Unless you make your profile private, you are open to bigotry at any time from anywhere. In the digital world, one user can present as many different users, which poses a unique threat to the mental health of a fat person who is visible. Further, for someone like me whose career is dependent upon visibility, making my profile private on a platform like Instagram is not feasible. This leads to choosing mental health over career opportunities.

The fantasy of consent in this case is, in fact, what makes the bigotry excusable and even desirable. Fatphobia is a form of oppression, and experiencing it is therefore not a choice. It is through the invocation of choice via the language of bootstrapping that the oppression is obscured. People cannot choose to experience fatphobia or not. We are all subject to the reality of its machinations. The idea of consent is imagined but is actually impossible given the terms.

Through positioning itself as a benevolent patriarch, the State gives itself permission to propagate violent behavior and in essence deputizes individual citizens to act on its behalf.

This brings us back to Dani Mathers, and how someone could so carelessly perpetrate such an obviously unacceptable act and then share it publicly without reservation with the expectation of social reward. These kinds of paradoxical behaviors abound in the case of social stigma. The culture allows individuals to act in unimaginably cruel ways while positioning them as innocuous. We are taught that fat women are a justifiable target through "war on obesity" rhetoric, media representations, and public-health campaigns.

These become the basis for our understanding of fat women (and in this case older women) as less than human. This dehumanization is internalized by individuals, and the dehumanization becomes the basis for cruelty.

Even though being unknowingly photographed naked is one of the most invasive and degrading experiences an individual can undergo at the hands of another person, it's important to realize that Mathers' behavior has bigger implications for fat women: *nowhere is safe to just exist.*

Fat women already opt out of public spaces like malls, beaches, restaurants, and, yes, gyms because we feel unsafe.

This is not a product of paranoia. It is a product of hypervigilance, an outlook informed by actual cruel behavior we have observed and experienced again and again.

We *rightly* fear being made fun of at any time.

We *rightly* fear being made to feel unwelcome.

We *rightly* fear being photographed without our consent.

Mathers' decision to dehumanize, publicly humiliate, and assault this unsuspecting woman shows the need not only for personal accountability but also for a cultural shift. We must stop asking people who are experiencing fatphobia to change their bodies. We must recognize culturally that fat shaming and fatphobia are expressions of bigotry, and that bigotry is a *social* problem, not an individual one.

Despite vociferous protestations and distancing from many people online, Dani Mathers' behavior didn't happen in a vacuum. She felt emboldened by the dominant discourse that positions fat women's bodies as public property, available for unabashed criticism and undeserving of basic rights, like privacy.

Wrestling with Consent (and Also Other Wrestlers)

JETTA RAE

A liability lawyer who hadn't grown up amid the normalization of pro wrestling—I don't know, maybe he joined a Frisbee golf team or some other such cult when he was young—would look at the career of Sting and see the potential for the hostile work environment payout of the century.

In 1989, he was locked inside an electrified steel cage. In 1990, a colleague dressed just like him tried to throw a fight on his behalf and cost him the World Title. In 1991, he was locked in a cage with seven other men until one of them was placed in an electric chair and electrocuted. In 1992, his opponent pulled out a live snake, which then proceeded to bite its owner. However, a crime in progress is not a sufficient reason to end a wrestling match, and as such Sting was forced to pin his opponent to end the fight, even as the snake wriggled and thrashed between them.

"And I haven't even gotten to 1996, when persistent impersonation of my client by the rival wrestling group New World Order caused such alienation with his coworkers that my client spent a year silently sulking in arena rafters," the lawyer would say. "It is my understanding you may not treat white men who believe in God like this in America."

This caricature of a lawyer I've dreamt up would be wrong. We can, we do; the capitalist system and the leftist movements that work to oppose it both have an opportunistic apathy for laborers of certain industries when it suits their narratives.

We assign a vulnerability to unskilled laborers, poor unfortunate souls just trying to make it in a world they never made. They desperately need the deliverance of our dialectic.

Meanwhile, workers with very specific skill sets—wrestlers, sex workers, migrant meat workers, those in industries that have long needed union representation and engagement— are just sort of left to the will of their niche markets. We internalize the capitalist notion of skills as inherently mobilizing. If you have a very specific skill set and only a few places that will pay you for it, that's not empowerment.

You still have to eat. Whether you can be fucked by a giant robot for hours on camera—which I'm told is not only uncomfortable, but also *boring*—or put snake wielders and cannibals in headlocks to save America from the forces of evil, this base need will always come in conflict with our cultural assumptions of consent.

It's dangerous to conflate the experience and skills needed to navigate very niche industries with *consenting* to do so.

I'll come back to that. Back to my imaginary lawsuit, there's a narratively damning flaw to Sting's anticipated payout, the sort that undoes a case not because it disproves it, but because it just *makes it look bad*: it wasn't a 400-pound man-creature or being set on fire by a Canadian vampire that ended Sting's retirement, but falling poorly in an otherwise mundane, normal wrestling match.

At Clash of the Champions 2015, Sting, 52, wrestled Seth Rollins, 26, for the World Title.

Rollins performed a "buckle bomb" on Sting: a move that consists of placing the opponent in a seated position on his shoulders, inverted, and launching them with a running start at the ring corner. It's important to emphasize that Sting fell "poorly" and didn't fall "wrong"; when you're falling backward into a vertical mass of metal and padding, you have a very limited margin of landing "right."

At the time, this was part of Rollins' regular repertoire (albeit later discontinued after he injured another wrestler with it a year later), a maneuver he workshopped on the road to make it safer and easier to perform without sacrificing the showmanship of commanding another man's body to gods of chaos and pain. And because of this ongoing effort, the men he wrestled agreed to have this move performed on them. They contracted the right muscles to be lifted up without too much struggle; they straightened their backs and shoulders for impact—beyond consent, they *collaborated.*

When we say wrestling is scripted, this incorrectly aligns it with films and television, where a fight or stunt coordinator meticulously plots out every blow and fall.

A high-profile wrestling match is like a competitive figure-skating routine: there are certain notes the competitors are expected to hit, but how they get from point to point is largely improvised, communicated through quick verbal exchanges, reading body language, and using the referee as a relayer. You've gotta do a few big moves, have the heel exploit a weakness and gloat, have the face rally after a beating to pump up the crowd, maybe destroy an announcer's table or fight in the front row—the rest is a gradient.

If you're in a main-event match, you've gotta get some of your signature moves in. If you don't, then your opponent looks weak for not *needing* those moves to defeat them, which then makes you look weak. Your promoter has a product he needs to look strong, and anyway none of you are employees. You're contractors, without health care or travel expense accounts. If you lose your job with that particular wrestling company after taking a big loss where you look ineffective in the ring, it will impact your ability to get work at other companies.

So, Sting *has* to take this move, or there'll be consequences, either from his boss or from the market. We can't and shouldn't conflate Sting and Seth Rollins' consent to cooperate to meet these expectations with being afforded the means to emphatically consent to the conditions of this workplace.

It is seductively simplistic to suggest that the tangible aspects of wrestling, or any job involving putting your body in harm's way, pose the greatest danger of harm—steel cages, spinning pile drivers, whips, or thrashing carnivores—but in some ways, it's the least visible exchanges of power that pose the greatest compromise.

Returning to my prior metaphor: the judge or defendant rebuffs our humble lawyer by saying, "Well, what business did your client have wrestling a guy half his age and willingly allowing Seth Rollins to perform this dangerous move on him?"

Pretty compelling. This probably does in our hapless liability lawyer's case. He goes back to trying to make condoms out of quinoa water or some shit. If it would ever even get that far. Pro wrestling has a long, documented history of collaborating with and promoting anti-leftist political establishments. Sting, devoutly religious and a stalwart icon of the sport, isn't likely going to go full-labor agitator near the end of public life.

And why should he? He's almost sixty, and he spent the prime of his life being kicked in the face for money. No organizations or institutions existed to protect him then, and none with any bargaining power have made a priority to speak up for him now.

Who we don't include casts commentary on who we do. It's one thing to take pride in being unexceptional; it's another for us as organizers to imply that we prioritize those people. Eventually we have to acknowledge that the allure of getting certain workers on board with labor and socialist platforms is because they hate their job.

This wholly imaginary model of niche industry consent to justify only sending our educated, eloquent rabble-rousers to speak to auto-industry and fast-food workers implies a very unkind and potentially undermining expectation that we have for those people's talents, capabilities, and desires.

To you and me, Sting taking that buckle bomb from Seth Rollins was the pinnacle of harm—it is likely the most equal-footed aspect of the whole enterprise, a moment where he and Rollins were equals collaborating, temporarily removed from the dynamics of exploitative promoters, industry norms, and consumer expectations that compel us to expect and react positively to a middle-aged man taking a bump that tore the shoulder of a man half his age.

Sting fought gods and monsters, in rings and in cages. He was also a laborer in an esoteric industry that tore his body apart, even as it venerated him as an icon with a legacy beyond reproach.

And frankly, his is one of the happier endings. The road to WrestleMania is paved with the shattered lives of people like Chyna, fired by her ex's new girlfriend and then blacklisted for doing porn, and Jim Harris, a Black man given the gimmick of a feral, Ugandan tribesman, who is part of a class action lawsuit alleging that World Wrestling Entertainment, Inc., has worked to conceal data around traumatic brain injuries.

If our movement is to survive the initial enthusiasm of the "Yes queen, resist" ideology of post–Donald Trump activism, these workers need to be invited to our meetings, to share their stories with other workers in other industries to develop the kind of solidarity-building understanding of shared struggle that would make our movement stronger than the impact of a Stinger Splash at minute forty-five of a main-event world championship match.

IN THE COMMUNITY

Games, Role-Playing, and Consent

KATE FRACTAL

I peer at the red-bordered name tag of the suited stranger with the top hat. The name is familiar from the sheet of paper I was just reading, I exclaim, "My dear old friend!" The stranger looks at my red-bordered name tag, checks his sheet of paper, and returns my greeting. He gives me a brief, warm hug and asks what brings me to this airship. I begin to tell him about my quest to find the lost amulet of steam, and wonder about the hug. Did this sign of affection indicate that my dear old friend was still pining for the one romantic summer I had read about on my sheet? Was the hug because he was attracted to me rather than the character I am playing? I am generally happy for hugs, but did he know that? Certainly, my character trusts his, but do I trust him?

This scene, while odd, is not unusual in the world of theater-style live-action role-playing (LARP) games. I've been involved in this community for about ten years, playing, organizing, and writing games. I'm not going to give a formal definition of what LARP is, a topic still argued about in the LARP community. Instead, I'll share my experience and stories from the strange and compelling worlds that I play in. These stories are a mix of true stories and invented details to better demonstrate the ideas.

You can imagine LARP as an extended improv theater sketch with no audience but the players. Or you can imagine a murder mystery dinner party where there isn't any murder, but there are a half-dozen mysteries. Or you might imagine a model UN meeting for the imaginary star league. You can imagine LARP as people dressed up as orcs hitting each other with foam swords, although that is a different style of LARP from the one I will be talking about. You can imagine anything you want, and if you act it out with other people and a few rules, building a shared imagination, I would call that LARP.

In LARP, people don't describe what their characters do; they just do it. Part of the fun is staying in character and being immersed in the simulated environment. This can complicate issues of consent and touch, as the opening example shows. Characters may be longtime lovers, but with players who have just met each other. A player who is a good friend might be the supervillain I am trying to defeat. Characters may be stalkers, murderers, or even just people who quickly resort to violence when threatened.

We all understand that we aren't actually going to hit each other (except possibly with foam swords) when our characters would, but should we hug when our characters would? How about kissing? Is it okay to back someone up against a wall when trying to intimidate their character? To stare intently into their eyes?

The consent issues in LARP go beyond just how and when we touch each other. A graphic description of violence done to a character you are inhabiting can be deeply hurtful. The potential for hurt feelings can bleed out from the games, especially for games that deal with serious real-world issues like discrimination or abuse. Being asked to take on certain roles can be triggering by itself. Ideally, we get to choose which interactions and experiences we want and which we don't.

As a theater LARPer, I play LARPs for the experience. I enjoy the intense emotions of triumph, connection, and surprise that can occur in LARP. In the context of a game where there aren't real-world consequences, I can also enjoy feelings of failure, guilt, and sorrow. I love the stories that come out of games, and the humor and drama that come up during game play. I deeply appreciate the chance to try things I can't do in real life, whether it's casting a magic spell, running a multi-national corporation, or actually having a date in high school.

> The game is set at a party of high school friends, years after graduation, and I am crying in the arms of my long-lost first love, who left me to pursue her career. The relief that she still wants me, despite the fact that in my youth and hurt I never returned her letters, is overwhelming. That relief and the sorrow for our lost time together are enough that tears form in my eyes. I am crying real tears for all that the scenario is fictional.
>
> In fact, the person whom I am hugging is a good friend, whom I am not romantically interested in. Is some of my emotion because I haven't seen this friend in months since she moved and had a baby, when we used to live down the street and see each other several times a week? Does the story give me permission to grieve for that lost closeness that otherwise might be deemed insignificant? Could I have had these cathartic tears without the hug?

> Without the uncertainty of knowing if this character wanted me?

Certainly, in order for me to have this experience, I needed a certain level of trust, not just of my fellow player, but also of the organizer and the space. I couldn't have experienced and processed this scene with blaring loud music in the background, nor with other people interrupting. The safer an environment feels, the greater the ability to enjoy the surprises of how the story unfolds. In this story, the surprise was that my high school sweetheart forgave me. Other times, I've been surprised to realize that another character was an android, or that the person I trusted had kidnapped my children. My most memorable surprise in a game was realizing, as we talked about the game afterward, that my character was actually undead.

As an organizer, I have a responsibility to provide a safe play space for my players. I set the stage and cast the players into roles based on information from the players about what they want. During the game, organizers will move through the game space and help players get what they want from the game, whether that is fun, striving to achieve goals, acting dramatically, or processing intense emotions. Often organizers help by clarifying game rules, but they may also identify a player who seems disengaged, bored, or distressed, and calmly ask if they want help.

The person running a game has typically written or read every character sheet that will be given to players and knows better than anyone else what can potentially happen in the game. For example, an organizer who knows that there might be physical violence in a game will explain the rules for how combat is resolved, possibly by rock–paper–scissors or comparing combat scores from the character sheets.

However, the organizer doesn't know exactly how a game is going to play out. I've run exactly the same game for different groups of players and had radically different experiences. *New Voices in Art* is a game where each player is a modern artist at the opening night of a gallery, with a piece of art and a single-sentence character sheet. With one group, the game was a deep introspection and sweet acknowledgment of the difficulties of being young and lacking confidence, with enough meaning and spoken internal monologues to fill two hours. Another group got bored of poking fun at the pretentiousness of modern art after only forty-five minutes. The game writing was the same, and the art pieces were similar. The big difference in the experience of the game was the group of players and what they brought to the game and wanted to get from it.

Given the magnitude of difference between individual runs of a game, my ability as an organizer to give players enough information for informed consent prior to the game is limited. I can make a reasonable guess as to what topics will come up, and how serious the game is, but I can never know for sure what will happen. Indeed, my adaption of a classic saying is "No game survives contact with the players."

> The game is supposed to be a light spy comedy. If you don't have a weapon, you can restrain but not kill another character. Two members of the People's Republic of Atlantis have restrained a merchant from El Dorado and are trying to figure out if the rumors of El Dorado's super-weapon development are true. The long-haired young man, laden with golden plastic necklace and rings, is sitting on a small wooden chair in the back corner of a college dorm's basement. When he tells the Atlanteans that

he doesn't know anything about any super weapon, the blue-shirted pair describe in graphic detail how they torture him. He screams "I don't know" and sobs "I'm just a merchant" and "Please stop doing this!" but they keep up their descriptions for half an hour until an organizer finds them, and explains that a character can't be restrained for more than ten minutes.

LARPs sometimes have as many as seventy players spread out over a college campus. Typically, there is an organizer for every ten players, but those organizers can't monitor all of the players all the time, especially in game that uses a lot of space. Moreover, it's impossible to tell if a player is enjoying an intense scene without breaking immersion. It seems likely that the young gold-bedecked player felt disturbed and violated by this scene. But it's also possible that the player was having fun with this interrogation scene. Certainly, "negative" emotions can be positive experiences, in the context of a game.

The genie, whom I had years earlier imprisoned in a lamp, hands me a magic spell card that reads "You feel more ___" and says "guilt." I forget that my character has magic resistance and immediately curl over double in guilt, and the genie walks off. Five minutes later, I go and ask an organizer how long the effect lasts, and am able to walk around again.

For me, the emotions and character development of that scene were fantastic. Indeed, my ability to manage my real-world emotions of shame and guilt grew significantly after the experience of "You feel more guilt" and "After five minutes, the feeling fades."

Do we have to abandon powerful experience like this one to ensure that people don't get hurt? In our world of imperfect communication and control, is consent culture doomed to be only an aspiration?

An organizer cannot take sole responsibility for the players' experiences in a game, nor for creating a consent culture, because a LARP isn't created solely by its organizer. Instead each LARP run is a shared experience crafted by the writers, organizers, and players together. Players can choose to take responsibility for discussing potential consent issues before the game starts, especially if they know with whom their character has a close relationship. Although, in some situations, such as one of the characters being in disguise, players may have to choose between surprise and pregame negotiations.

A dozen adults dressed as though they were kids sit around the room looking over their papers, while they wait for the final players to arrive. A gray-haired man dressed in a T-shirt, shorts, and a baseball cap, character sheet in hand, approaches a woman with her long dark hair put up in pigtails. He greets her and introduces himself, as well as his character, a favor which she returns. Then he goes on. "So I'm reading here that my character has a crush on yours, and I don't want to make you uncomfortable. Also, he seems to be rather impulsive. I ask before giving hugs, but this character wouldn't. How do you feel about me coming up and hugging you in the game?"

She tilts her head and thinks for a moment. "Sure!" she says, and then clarifies. "But don't pick me up off my feet, and stop when I ask."

Organizers can help facilitate consent by providing time for one-on-one negotiations prior to game start. Traditionally, before the game starts, organizers will have a round of introductions where everyone says who they are playing. Increasingly, I've seen organizers ask people to include in their introduction how comfortable they are with casual touch.

> "I'm Tom, the ship's cat," says the young woman dressed in all gray with matching cat ears on her head. "I'm fine with petting, except on my chest, and I like scritches behind the ears. You may try to rub my belly, but I may scratch, in character. Do not actually try to pick me up; just say, 'I pick you up.'" She nods at the man in the captain's uniform next to her.
>
> He gives his intro. "I'm Captain Ahab. Shaking hands or tapping me for attention is fine, but please don't hug me, unless we already hug each other out in the real world." Then he turns to the next player.
>
> "I'm Avery, the cook," says the apron-clad player. "I'm happy with casual touch, including hugs. You are unlikely to make me uncomfortable, unless you are trying to."

Before game start is an excellent time for organizers to go beyond explaining the game's rules and set expectations for what constitutes acceptable behavior in a game. They can remind players to respect each other's boundaries and to make self-care a priority. If they know that something is a trigger spot for a player, they can explicitly name the off-limit element.

Thirty people dressed as pirates sit on the benches near a soccer field. The organizer has just walked around the edge of the field to show the players the extent of the island they are about to be stranded on. "Now, I know you are all blood-thirsty pirates, but in this game we do have some limits." The organizer continues. "If you want to interrogate another pirate after winning combat, just say that you are going to do that and fade to black. Do not describe what you are doing in detail! Also, there will be no cannibalism in this game. I know it's plausible in the setting, but just don't do it."

Additionally, organizers can introduce communication techniques to allow people to quickly indicate a boundary. Some LARP communities use the safe words "brake" and "cut." "Brake" indicates out of character that a scene is pushing a boundary and other players should back off. The word "cut" is used to indicate that something has gone wrong and the game needs to stop until the issue has been resolved.

In a game where players know about safe words, the player of the El Dorado merchant from earlier could have said "brake" to tell the Atlantean players that he, not just his character, was uncomfortable with the scene. Of course, players also need to remember the safe words, be comfortable using them, and respect their meaning when someone else uses them.

While immersion is a goal for LARP, so are fun, comfort, and imagination. Games and creativity thrive with limits and boundaries. A totally unconstrained LARP would have no common world for players to share. Having limits based on the safety of the players is obviously important when we are talking about physical safety and should be the same when we talk about emotional safety.

You might say that developing a consent culture is choosing to value the safety and comfort of every participant over the most immersive, in-character, or intense experiences for some participants. However, I believe that, in the long run, valuing safety and comfort creates more opportunities for intense immersive play. A player who is comfortable using "brake" and has that safe word respected isn't going to disrupt immersion by screaming, crying, or shoving to get out of an uncomfortable situation, nor will they walk out of a game halfway through, leaving dangling plot threads for other players. Players who trust that their boundaries will be respected are more willing to take a risk and play a more intense game. I know that when I'm deciding whether or not to play an emotionally intense game, I look at who the organizers are and make the decision based on how much I trust them.

Ultimately, consent culture is not made by any one person, but rather is something we all have a say in. As organizers and leaders, we can normalize asking for consent by providing convenient times and ways to do so, while remembering that consent culture also means trusting the players to create the game that they want. As players, we can prioritize communicating our boundaries and desires, and taking care of ourselves. All of us can support rather than shame people who break out of character to express their limits, and we can all thank people when they ask for what they want.

Trouble, Lies, and White Fragility: Tips for White People

CINNAMON MAXXINE

Here's some advice for white people on how to center consent in their interactions with black and brown folks, by a salty queer black femme who's tired of your shit.

On gratitude and opportunities

I often find myself being overly grateful when a white person offers me work. I also feel like I can't turn it down, negotiate pay, or basically have any say around any of the work or opportunities offered to me. If I do, it makes me seem ungrateful. This is, however, a demonstration of the ways my interactions with white people end up coercive rather than consensual, filled with landmines of social niceties I'm expected to perform.

A few years ago, I was doing some video editing work for my white roommate who had a falling-out with one of their employees. Instead of keeping me out of it altogether, they complained to me all the time about the situation, how they felt unsupported by the community for continuing to talk to the ex-employee. Eventually, it came down to them losing their shit over my still being in communication with the ex-employee. White fragility and unspoken, coercive expectations of how I was supposed to behave meant I lost income and, when they kicked me out, my home.

White people—do not ever demand a black or brown person grovel on their knees in praise or do much more to show you they're grateful other than a simple thank you. Do not expect us to kiss your ass as a thank you. Do not offer work or labor to a black or brown person with the expectation that you deserve something in return, because honestly, you don't. Black and brown people need more work and more income than white folks do. If you have a job opening or need a job done, there is absolutely no reason it should be going to anyone else. Part of centering consent means ensuring that black and brown folks have financial power.

On choosing sides

White people—you should never ask a black or brown person to choose sides between people in order for them to keep their job. Especially if it's a personal issue. Don't make them feel like they have to choose sides, agree with you, or anything else. It's actually really wrong and toxic to make a black or brown person feel like their job, their home, or their access to community is on the line if they don't agree with you. People cannot give true consent if they don't feel safe to say no.

On "borrowing"

When a brown person comes to you and says, "Your artwork looks a lot like this thing I told you about or that I'm working on," you actually need to listen and think about the ways in which you may have straight-up stolen their ideas, or at the very least been inspired by their work (let's be honest, though; more often than not, it's just stolen).

Which is why something you can do to create a more consensual dynamic is credit and pay people of color. If you get called out for doing something problematic along these lines, such as wearing appropriative clothing or not telling your boss that your brown coworker really finished that project, or if your artwork looks exactly like this black person's art, it's literally never too late to own up. It's also never too late to give credit where credit is due, and/or to compensate someone.

White people —stop stealing ideas from people of color! Like, for real. White people do this every day, from their fashion choices to stealing ideas worth money. Be mindful of how you're taking credit from black and brown people. White people consistently steal our ideas and pass them off as their own and even trick themselves into thinking that the idea is theirs. Every. Damn. Day.

On compensation

White people consistently steal our ideas and then profit from them, sometimes in really big ways. Black and brown people don't always get those opportunities. As black and brown people, we always have to go above and beyond to make things happen for ourselves, to get that raise, to get this job, to get paid equally, to get that room, or simply to make ends meet. It's really infuriating to see a white person profit and benefit from your community or you personally while you can't even eat every day, or pay rent, or go to school, or whatever it may be.

The work I usually do is gig-style work and one-offs—this writing thing here, go-go dancing there, a DJ thing, video editing, things like that. What happens a lot is that white people expect extras from me, things they didn't pay for or that were not previously negotiated. Sometimes, it's okay, but generally it's really annoying, rude, and just all-around exhausting. Not only are you pushing my boundaries, but I also have to do the work of either:

◆ asking you for more money (which I often won't do because history tells me I'm not worth it as a black femme)

◆ talking to you about it and most likely having to break down race dynamics, power dynamics, class dynamics, and other shit, which is also labor

◆ letting it go and worrying about whether or not you knew what you were doing, while also worrying that you're going to do it to someone else

White people—don't expect black and brown folks do your emotional labor, budgeting, or time sheets for you. Know what you're asking, know what's fair compensation, and negotiate fairly.

On clear negotiation

Check the ways in which you use people of color for their labor. Do not hire a person of color for one job and expect them to do a bunch of extra labor for cheap or free. Sometimes, this looks like hiring a brown person as an editor but then asking them to stay late at the office for free because it needs to be cleaned. Sometimes this looks like hiring a black femme as a receptionist, then spending chunks of time talking about how you "deserve" to date people of color and you don't understand why brown people won't just give you a chance. That's emotional labor, it's unprofessional, and it's also really exhausting.

Be considerate of the space you expect people to work in as well. You need to make sure the workspace is clean. First and foremost, you can do this by cleaning up after yourself.

Don't ask people of color to clean up after you, your animals, or your friends, without additional compensation. Keep shared spaces free of poop and pee if you have pets. Don't expect people of color to clean up after you. Don't even ask them to, unless you're explicitly hiring them to do that work. And pay extra.

White people—do not ever take advantage of the labor of people of color. Seriously. When people do labor for you, especially physical or emotional, you respect the hell out of that. It's actually a fucking gift.

On ownership

Do not ignore being called out (or called in, or whatever) especially when the issue has to do with race or any other fucked-up ism. Not only does it show that you are not to be trusted, but it also shows that you are totally okay with being a racist, classist, ableist creature...and that you have absolutely no intention of changing.

Want to show that you care about community and people of color and supporting everyone? Apologizing and holding yourself accountable are absolutely necessary first steps, especially when you have more social capital or hold some sort of power (like as an employer or a performer).

When you make a mistake and fuck up, when you get called out, when you're told by a friend or community member that you did wrong, you listen. You don't ignore it, you don't try to cover it up, you don't delete the comments or posts, you don't say that the other person was crazy; you shut up and listen. When you ignore it, you're basically telling everyone you don't care and you did nothing wrong. When you delete comments or posts, you're saying you don't want to listen to other people. In fact, you're saying that you won't be challenged and you're actively silencing other people. When you delete things with no comment or statement, you're refusing accountability, which is especially concerning when you hold financial and social power over marginalized people.

Additionally, as a white person, you don't get to cry "Poor me! That person bullied me!" That is a tactic white people have used for a very long time to scare other white people into believing that all people of color are bullies and scary, mean, rude, bad, terrible people who shouldn't be trusted. If your first response to being challenged, called out, called in, or whatever regarding an issue with a person of color is to say they made you feel scared or unsafe, or otherwise put it off on them and how insecure they made you feel, then you really need to reflect on why that's your go-to. I'm here to tell you that the root of it is fucked-up racism that you really need to work on, especially if you care about consent.

On shutting up

Do not silence people of color. At all. Ever. For any reason. During every interaction people of color have to weigh, edit, re-weigh, and re-edit every single thing they may want to say. If a person of color is talking to you about any personal information, any oppression they've experienced, whether or not they're trying to gently call you out, chances are they're editing themselves. They're also probably going out on a huge limb to even have this conversation with you.

Instead of silencing someone who is already taking a huge risk (the personal blow of being silenced by a white person you consider a friend is heart-wrenching) in talking to you, consider their words. Actually absorb what they're saying. Take a minute to self-reflect on what is making you so uncomfortable and sit with that. Figure out why defending yourself is more important than the damage you've caused someone you claim to care about. Consider what happens when someone who is repeatedly silenced reaches out. The trust and care that is put into another interaction that could realistically turn into violence being enacted against them yet again. Do some research on your own on how to handle your white privilege. Talk to other anti-racist white people about it.

Many times silencing people isn't simply ignoring a friend of color who told you that you hurt them. It can manifest as flagging a person's post on Facebook because you didn't like the content or it said something that you disagreed with. It can manifest as kicking them out of your house for telling you black and brown people don't owe you anything. Or it could be firing them because they dare questioned why their white coworker always gets to leave early to pick up her kids but they always have to stay late, even though that means their kids have to take public transit alone. It might be telling people that a black person made you feel unsafe so you can discredit that person and therefore no one will listen to them.

We, black and brown people, often have few to no safe spaces where can speak freely and safely. What people of color have to say holds value, and you need to unlearn that your voice is the most important.

White people—you need to unlearn that your emotions hold the most value. You need to hear the damage, pain, and trauma imperialism, white colonialism, white supremacy cause black and brown people daily. You need to learn to see the generational trauma people of color are forced to carry their entire lives, you need to educate yourself on your own time, and you need to learn to sit with your uncomfortability and change your behaviors and actions.

All of these things interact with consent, because if you don't feel safe to say no, your yes doesn't mean anything. By working on making space for black and brown people in your life, you can combat the idea that your consent trumps theirs. You can demonstrate to black and brown folks that you care about not coercing them into labor they don't want to do. Consent culture cannot truly exist without that understanding and respect.

Sleeping with Fishes: A Skinny Dip into Sex Parties

ZEV UBU HOFFMAN

An anxious excitement hangs over the group. They've made it through the gated door, tucked between the rhinestone-encrusted cowboy shop crammed with epic belt buckles and studded-leather goods...and, well, a credit union. Through a second set of doors, they begin to hear music. A line of costumed freaks ascends a glowing red staircase ahead of them, each waiting for their chance to reach the top and witness the promised sensual decadence they've glimpsed in late-night Hollywood softcore.

Our group are newcomers. Having only what they've learned from porn, erotica, late-night sex scandal spin pieces, and hearsay, they assume they're in for a sex buffet of sorts, a world where men with greasy hair and low-cut shirts prowl around women dressed in this year's selection of sexy Halloween costumes.

They expect facetious smiles, dead-eyed stares, and the pushy attitudes they have become accustomed to from dating apps and the local sports bar pick-up scene.

When people are invited to a sex party, they imagine something out of *Eyes Wide Shut* or *Caligula*. They expect a hedonistic explosion of desire and pleasure, populated with beautiful people with toned bodies, where rules are secondary to sensuality and fantasies become real.

Or something like that, anyway.

The reality, in my experience, is perhaps more like *Shortbus*, if we're to reference a movie: awkward, funny, emotionally intense, erotic, challenging, bonding. As someone who not only attends sex parties but also helps host them, I have seen relationships form, flare up, and fade out, sometimes within a night. A sex party is a strange alchemy: a space where possibility can be omnipresent for some, but where others can get left behind.

As they reach the top of the stairs they get a glance of the wonderful costumed abyss that awaits them. Our explorers encounter a sea of aquatic animals adorned in sequins, latex, leather, spandex, and repurposed EVA foam (i.e., dirty old yoga mats). A large salmon swims hard against the current, or rather the mass of aquatic people piled together blocking the hallway to the rest of the party. A pair of manatees grind hard and passionately against the wall as a bloom of jellyfish, draped in tulle, makes its way past the shrimp-adorned host, who is trying, with the assistance of the salmon, to get people to stop hanging out in the entryway.

Even an under-the-sea play party has to respect the fire code.

A gaggle of merpeople, mostly naked, and immaculately painted, talk to a fully grown man stuffed inside of a child's shark costume. His long pale legs shoot downward. That's me, by the way. In a world of immaculate creativity, I am the one stuffed inside a onesie made for a three-year-old.

The space that I'm most familiar with, the one I became myself in, has a code of conduct—a community-sourced group of guidelines and rules that have been formulated for maximum comfort. It's a list that's on the website where you buy the tickets, and it's also posted in the front hallway. We go over the list with everyone, no matter how many times they've come to the party—it serves not only as a reminder of the boundaries of the space but also as a checkpoint for partygoers so they can reflect on where their head and heart are at.

DO
+ Be creative about how you dress.
+ Contribute when and where you can.
+ State your boundaries.
+ Play safely and consensually.
+ Have sensible safe-sex practices.
+ Respect our space and each other.
+ Clean up after yourself.

DON'T
+ Linger unaccompanied in play spaces.
+ Cruise aggressively (even if they are really cute).
+ Get too intoxicated.
+ Take photographs.
+ Use your cell phone.
+ Gossip about what goes on here.

Each play party community has a different set of these, whether they call them rules, a charter, a code of conduct, or shared values. Some parties care about a dress code, others insist on safer sex, still others don't allow substance use at all. It's important to work out what the terms of engagement are for each party, not only so you know how to behave, but also so you know what to expect.

Of course, differences exist between communities. Some, like the polyamorous and swinger scenes, might assume similar values by the average person but would likely differ based on their specific contexts. Polyamory has become more of a blanket term to describe a variety of relationships and styles, all with the focus of having multiple partners (often romantic or sexual in nature). Swingers, on the other hand, have historically tended toward being closely tied to the nuclear family, often married couples looking for a good time while avoiding additional emotional contact. Not that it's a hard-and-fast rule, of course—there are other iterations as well, including asexual non-monogamous people and swingers who do form emotional connections but limit them to the party space.

Assuming cultural norms can be an issue as well. A BDSM party may lead the inexperienced kinkster to assume that all men at the event are dominant or that all women are submissive. This would be a grave mistake informed by media depictions of what kinky sex looks like—one should always ask instead of jumping to conclusions! Additionally, while some parties may not make a point about spelling this out, it's also important not to assume people's genders or pronouns. Asking is a good rule of thumb, as is letting the person know that they don't have to answer if they don't want to. Offering an out is an easy way to extend acknowledgment that no is a fair answer.

In the hallway waits a pair of moderately experienced wondersluts. They have a history of play parties in their past (although they are new to this one) and a long list of preconceptions and expectations based on different parties with different structures. They've been to swingers' parties, Burning Man, and campouts with friends that blend from casual hanging out to casual sex and back again.

The newbies, having intermingled and mixed within the space, have quickly found this place to be welcoming and inviting. People approach, introduce themselves, and engage in lively conversation, but without the handsiness and pushy attitudes they were expecting.

Although some flirtatious attitude is often present, smiles with hidden agendas aren't nearly as prevalent as the newcomers were expecting. People are flirty, but they don't make a move unless consent is negotiated, often verbally and directly. The newbies find this a little frustrating at first—of course the super hot merdude they meet in the entry can kiss them! Why would he even bother asking? Have you seen him? He can have whatever he wants!

They learn quickly the errors in their thinking when one newbie touches the merdude without that negotiation, and is politely but firmly reminded to ask first.

If you attend play parties, there is a good chance that at some point you are going to cross someone's boundaries. What really matters, once this happens, is how you deal with it. Don't try to pretend that it didn't happen or try to shift the blame onto them. Give them the power to choose how to deal with it. A rap sheet of your mistakes is worth less than the recourse you pursued to take ownership of those mistakes—while it is irresponsible to expect that boundaries will never be crossed, it is about how you manage being told that you fucked up that matters. Apologize, ask what you can do to help others feel safe, and then do it. If you need to process how uncomfortable you feel about having crossed a boundary, find a close friend to discuss it with respectfully, anonymously (for the person you hurt), and without blame, rather than asking the person whose boundary you crossed to do that work for and with you.

Not far from the newbies, a similar interaction is taking place. A tall, dapper pufferfish, one of our wondersluts, bends down slightly. "Can I kiss you?" he asks the woman he's been chatting up, a hipster Ariel with long red hair, boxy framed glasses, a plaid shirt, and a fishtail.

"No, sorry, I'm just not up for that right now," she responds with a small smile, looking up into his grey-spine-covered face.

He smiles back. "No worries. Would you like to keep chatting?"

"Sure!" Ariel beams, and the two continue to flirt and laugh.

Thus continues the dance of consensuality, a world of negotiation, and respect of boundaries. We must acknowledge that a sex party is not outside of the realm of privilege or power, and stay aware that we must take verbal and nonverbal cues into account. If someone is saying yes to you but moving away or not meeting your eyes, that may well be a no. I recommend assuming a no over assuming a yes—it's better to confirm consent than it is to violate a boundary in your presumption.

Granted, there are parties and events that cater more to the implied consent, or consent by association, fantasy—the idea that by showing up, you've already agreed to certain behaviors. Different strokes for different folks! The problem occurs when this model of implied consent becomes the face of sex culture, without any structure for implementing rules or agreements. These parties are often unstable, run a higher risk of boundary crossing, and have a history for victim blaming, especially if the perpetrator is part of the crew. These parties are not part of consent culture, nor the sex-positive scene. They are, by nature, closely related and tied to rape culture. Funnily enough, if a party seeks to mimic rape culture, even within a container, it runs the risk of perpetuating the same behaviors. We should therefore question how to create a space for such fantasies without underlining the same power dynamics that exist in society at large...and whether that is even possible.

When a party focused on implied consent ends, the partygoers leave to a society that mirrors and emphasizes those values—the idea that it's better to ask forgiveness than permission. If we truly want to foster a consent culture, we must encourage people to take these clear discussions about consent out of the bedrooms and into their everyday lives.

At the end, the lights will come up, changing the luscious red velvet walls to shabby fabric haphazardly nailed in place. That one piece of painter's tape stuck above the door to the dance floor that has been there for years will suddenly become visible. The final orgasms have been had. Lube-stained and happy, the newcomers stumble down the street with only three shoes between them.

I have a fondness for the space in the harsh light—a creative wonderland jumbled together with duct tape, staples, and tacks. Literal trash turned into classy decor, the belief that what can't be fixed with lighting can be covered by art or fabric. Here, I am a permanent resident. At the end, only the mess and I will remain. I step over a torn sequined gown tangled around a discarded pair of panties, all sitting in a sticky pool of energy drink. I brush my teeth and take a shower, then make my way to reclaim my bedroom. The "pink room" is a small hidden nook filled with beds, just off the dance floor and great for people looking for something a little more private. I pick my favorite of the three mattresses laid out on the floor. With gloves, I reach into the crevices of the bed, pulling out condoms, wrappers, and torn lube containers. The soiled pink sheets come off; towels get laid over various wet spots. Finally I pull out my bedroll—a trick shown to me by a friend who lived in this room before me. Everything I need to sleep—blankets, pillows, top sheet, bottom sheet—all laid out as they should be, rolled up for a quick bed making. The whole thing takes me a total of about five minutes...ten if I'm tired.

Like the bedroll, a sex party should be a clean, safe place, with everything thing you need to keep yourself, and anyone who might be cuddling up with you, comfortable, happy, and healthy. They need to know for certain that there isn't an unpleasant unknown hidden underneath those sheets. Your intentions, like your bed, need to be a known space. They need to be able to see that you have the necessary pillows to fit their comfort, that your blankets and sheets are clean and inviting (I mean, unless otherwise specified). They need to know there aren't going to be any unwanted surprises stabbing, bumping, groping, or poking. This can only happen through communication, being both flexible and willing to work with what happens, good and bad, and remaining gracious, willing to listen, and firm in your own boundaries. If you stay on top of this, and take care of the physical and emotional safety of those around you, your dreams can very much come true.

I do have one boundary request, though, across the board.

Seriously, people: stop leaving your fucking shoes at the party.

Sex Is a Life Skill: Sex Ed for the Neuroatypical

SEZ THOMASIN

We are having some...issues with one of our students, and we'd like you to come and talk to them about what is and is not... appropriate.

As a sex educator, this phone conversation opener always rings alarm bells for me. Often, it's a senior teacher or head of year inviting my sympathy as she deals with an inconsiderate young person who has had the temerity to come out as queer while still at school, forcing teachers to address their own and the other students' rampant homophobia or transphobia. My job, she hopes, will be to come in and talk to the kid about "toning it down" for their "own good" (and the school's convenience; much easier for the staff if the kids stay in the closet).

However, when this sort of situation comes up, I have a script. I immediately offer bespoke LGBT+ awareness training for staff, I provide information about local LGBT youth groups, and I link them into national strategies for tackling gender- and sexual orientation–based bullying. This is my wheelhouse. I know how to flip the script so that suddenly what they are getting is not "Operation put the kid back in the closet" but a much-needed wake-up call about their equality and diversity responsibilities as a school.

This, I know how to do.

The first time I got a call like that from a school for students with learning and developmental disabilities, though, it was different.

The teacher who called me that day was not concerned about students' homosexuality; she was concerned that the students had any sexuality at all. Yes, a group of teenagers with problems understanding social boundaries had shocked their teachers by displaying sexual attraction toward each other. My job was to come in and tell them to stop it. After all, these kids could not possibly really understand what they were saying and doing, she told me; they were just copying what they'd seen on TV. Some of them had an academic age of five; they could not possibly understand or consent to a sexual relationship.

Of course, what the well-meaning woman telling me all this on the phone did not know was that I *was* one of these kids. Being autistic, I have what is called a learning disability (I call it a processing difference). Shockingly, I also fuck. Despite my acute hypersensitivity (and sometimes near total imperviousness) to touch, and my frankly laughable flirting skills, I have a long-term partner and I really enjoy sex. For some neurotypical people, this is a mindfuck. I get that: for a long time, it was a bit of a mindfuck for me.

As someone who started secondary school in the 1990s, I was of the generation who got a LOT of rather panicky, amateur, doom-laden sex education. Suddenly teachers for whom "Don't do it till you're married and then take the pill if you don't want ten babies" had done very nicely had to talk about the fact that teenagers might already be doing it, and doing it suddenly carried risks that could not be sorted out with a quiet, shamefaced trip to a clinic. AIDS panic was in full swing.

So, did we get lessons touching on loving relationships? Non-heterosexual sex? Consent and boundaries? No chance. We talked about AIDS, death, pregnancy, despair, and condoms. Lots of condoms. Girls were taught that the absolute jackpot when it came to boyfriends was a guy who would use a condom. Boys were taught that using a condom made them an absolute fucking hero. A hero of fucking. The Fuckboy Wonder.

I don't know what a neurotypical person would have made of all that, but my autistic little brain took away the following precepts:

- The idea of sex is to not get pregnant and not get HIV.
- Use a condom.
- As a girl, if you have a boyfriend, it is your job to withhold sex until he agrees to wear a condom.
- When he wears a condom, you say yes.
- Boys get erections. They are the ones who need the sex.
- If a condom breaks your life is probably over, but you can get a morning-after pill, which will give you a fighting chance of not getting pregnant.
- Obtaining the morning-after pill will be both a thrilling race against time and the most mortifying experience of your life.
- So use a damn condom
- You are probably going to get pregnant.
- You are probably going to get HIV.
- You are a cisgender, heterosexual girl, by the way.
- You want a boyfriend. One with condoms.
- Don't forget about condoms.

As a result, when a guy did show some sexual interest in me, and when we managed to level up to boyfriend-and-girlfriend status despite my near total silence in public and unholy terror of eye contact, the idea that I was supposed to enjoy the sex did not really cross my mind.

I did enjoy sex, though: I liked the feeling of accomplishment. Look what I could make his penis do! Look how happy I could make him! Who knew my vagina could get all capacious like that? It turned out he was a decent bloke who really wanted to make me happy too. Which, given the standards presented in sex education, made him some kind of miracle Prince Charming. We took it slow, he worked hard to turn me on to the extent that my vagina did the required stretching and squishing, and he agreed to all my stipulations about ultra-safe, name-brand condoms. I'd seen enough sex scenes in movies to make the right noises at the right times. I liked the way those noises made him feel good.

I did not think I was missing out on anything: We were using condoms. He was getting off. I was not pregnant; neither of us seemed to have HIV. That's what good sex was, wasn't it? I was totally winning at sex.

So, the first time I kissed a girl, the sensory overload was all the more intense for being totally unexpected. My boyfriend, who really was quite the gentleman, could just about get me going enough—with a *lot* of cunnilingus—for penetration to be relatively hassle free. When a girl I was drunkenly sexy-dancing with at a party grabbed my hair and stuck her tongue down my throat, I damn near came on the spot. I was absolutely terrified. And delighted. And angry. Nobody had told me this. Why had nobody told me this? What *was* this?

My experience of sex education would probably have been even less informative if my autism had been diagnosed while I was at school. While the lessons were at best inadequate, there was a basic assumption that I would one day be sexually active, even though I was a withdrawn and introverted loner. Teenagers who are sent to special schools are taught "life skills." Telling time, cooking a meal, money math, personal hygiene—all of these will be covered on a daily basis for most of their formal education. Sex? The lucky few will get a video vaguely hinting at where babies come from. "Growing up" will be briefly discussed in a science lesson. The only time any more action will be taken is if (when) the students act on the sort of feelings any teenager will start to experience.

That's when I get those phone calls. Those requests to just get these poor, unfortunate children to stop doing what they can't possibly understand. Not with their mental capacity.

And the first time I got a phone call like that, I went to the school and I told them. I haven't stopped telling them.

I tell the kids all the things I was angry I'd not been told. We talk about sexual pleasure. About different kinds of orgasm. About penises and vaginas and what our bodies might do when we feel sexy. We talk to them about saying no and saying yes. We eat snacks and we talk about how it would not be okay to force-feed anyone a snack they did not want to eat just then. We talk about the ways our bodies and faces might be saying no, and how we listen to all the ways we tell each other what is and isn't okay. We talk about whom to talk to if something doesn't seem right or someone is making us feel unsafe. We talk about rape; we talk about abuse. Yes, we talk about HIV and pregnancy and condoms. We talk about gender and sexuality and all the different ways people can have sex. We talk about asexuality.

And they are never too young, and they are never too disabled, and—as people who have very often had their autonomy violated, as teenagers with crushes and fantasies, and changing bodies, as people with long-term conditions controlled by medication—they, more than most, will under-stand all of these things, if only someone takes the time to teach good sexual health and well-being as a life skill.

And sometimes, just sometimes, the teachers start to understand too.

Afterword

CAROL QUEEN

I should have been able to tackle this afterword easily. I have about a thousand things to say about consent; Kitty has brought great voices to the task at hand, and I know that when readers set this book down, they'll have the skills and perspectives they need to make change, in their lives and in society. Grasping and practicing consent has ramifications in many more realms than the sexual—all manner of oppressive behavior is predicated on ignoring consent, which is a justice issue in every way. (A recent iteration much in the news: doxxing.)

But it *is* about sex too, of course, how we experience sex inextricably linked to it, so I know this collection of insights and challenges will effect that kind of change for readers' own body-to-body lives: bring them more pleasure, support their boundaries. In the aggregate, our own singular experiences with (and without) consent themselves are paving stones on the road. They help move the culture along its arc to the day when sex can be pleasurable for anyone who wants to have it, and we can *all* say yes as well as no...and perhaps even maybe! (Those feelings of *maybe*, fraught and contingent as they are, are where the really exciting work lies. When *maybe* is never an equivocal dodge but always opportunity and means to get closer to our own enthusiastic, passionate *yes*—what a day that will be.)

That's not the world in which I grew up, although consent culture isn't as new as many imagine it is. The seeds of this discussion had already been planted and begun to flower by the mid-1970s, when I was in college. If you were attuned to feminist discourse, it was even then part of the way we talked about sex, though admittedly, there was way more then being said about breaches of consent than about frank sexual desire...and even than about consent itself. I don't remember hearing the term *consent* used regularly until I came to San Francisco to get my doctorate in sexology, exploring all the sexual and/or eroticized subcultures I could find, and discovered that within BDSM, consent was talked about all the time. Achieved? Maybe not always. But taken seriously, yes, way more than in mainstream culture.

In the 1970s I was exposed to the view that rape is always about power, not sex and desire, and in the world documented by Susan Brownmiller, maybe that's accurate. But that's not the limit of what I saw over the course of several decades of sexual exploration. Even now—and I wonder whether somehow that "power-over" definition influences this—guys who want sex and don't get a clear yes will say it *was* consensual, not rape, tangled up in not only their own entitlement and desires but also the insidious dark-alley definitions of what it means to be a rapist. Both the times I know I was raped, it was so much more complicated than that, and all the many times it could be argued I hadn't given clear consent—boozed up or stone-cold sober and curious but contingent—all those other times were even *more* complicated. I know as a formerly young woman whose most profound access to sex information was through *having actual sex* that I never got enough support to be a good sexual communicator; neither did most of the people with whom I had sex. I know as an older woman who's devoted her life to learning those skills that most other people still don't get them. We can talk about consent till we can't talk any more, but without a way to *teach* people about consent, not just conceptually but in the body and in the voice, we won't arrive at the consent culture we seek.

I also know the consent issue isn't as gendered as we usually imply it is. My first consentless and eye-contact-less sexual experience—the first one I called a rape to myself—was "with" a man, it's true. But my second one was perpetrated by a woman. I'm pretty sure if she knew I considered it a rape, she would be horrified; I know I was, when I acted like a happy puppy at a sex party one time and touched a man who hadn't given me permission to be part of the scene. I feel lucky that the guy spoke up: it broke the gendered spell of the "men only want one thing" message I received from my mother. Half the time, I wanted that thing too. The rest of the time, it was just…just…*complicated.*

The exact same physical act can be experienced as a good (or at least okay) sexual experience or a consent violation; acting on your own desire or interest and figuring that interest is shared by another person is a recipe for fun, awkwardness, "we need to talk," or, yes, rape. Consent violations are so much easier to recognize as such when they're inappropriate: rude, too sudden, in a context of insufficient interpersonal connection, violent. But they happen when people are in love, in relationships, even in the mood.

I have to tell you, I don't find it remotely surprising that lots of people cannot intuit what's appropriate, given the crappy sex education most of us have had (and the fact that so many people's workaround is studying porn as though it's documentary film). When *not being stopped* is conflated with active consent, clearly that's a problem. In the world in which

I've lived, an even bigger culprit than acted-out power has been the failure of sex education to equip us for real-time sexual experience. Consent, especially enthusiastic, is just not possible without access to sex information: this, in fact, is one of the greatest barriers consent culture activists must tackle.

This is not to say I excuse perpetrators their actions, but it does make me mutter that school board members, abstinence-only believers, and parents ought more often to be charged as accessories to these crimes.

So over and over I have sat down to write about consent and found myself all the way out in the weeds. I have wrestled with the current discourse about the role of disinhibitors. Of course we should all be able to get blasted and stay completely safe! Wouldn't that be nice? And taking legal steps to spell out that an incapacitated person can't give consent is a significant step. But I want to remind all my young friends who believe in a culture of safety that just as it's hard to say an empowered *yes* or a fierce *no* when we're fucked up, it's even harder to effectively kick someone in the nuts in that condition. What I mean is, we have not yet *created* a culture of safety. I'm pretty sure my speaking this way won't be popular in all corners, and that's not even the first reason that this is hard to write about; much more challenging to me is the gap between any ability I have to address the now accepted understandings of a generation with no patience to wait for a better future with my old-school skills sourced in the brisk advice of old-school feminist *Realpolitik*.

But these complications and contradictions aren't enough to account for this unaccustomed grip of writer's block. All year I kept repeating to myself, "I have a thousand things to say about consent!" And then I'd get distracted and fail to write the afterword that Kitty was expecting.

And more often than not, I'd get distracted by something having to do with consent...aaaaaand Donald Trump.

Physicists posit that there exist parallel worlds, and it was tempting to think in 2016 that we had fallen through a cosmic veil and landed in one of them. In that world, I had writer's block and a serial sexual abuser was running for president. Speculative fiction at its finest!

Then, as I am sure you know (unless you somehow managed to escape back to the other dimension where we have a lady president), that guy was elected.

The election cycle was so full of sex referents that it became perfectly (and, to me, fascinatingly) clear that sex is a different, more public issue in the twenty-first century than it was in the twentieth. (And it was pretty *damn* public then, at least in my day, my darling young one.) Like the contrast between Miss Kitty on *Gunsmoke* and Dolores on *Westworld*, that's how different. Those issues that were up for me and other young feminists forty years ago—the glass ceiling, sexual harassment, rape, and assault—have become centered in mainstream discourse. They aren't just being discussed in alternative culture spaces any more. Too, *most* women have experience with unwanted sexualization and touch, and the scenarios that Trump's accusers sketched out resonate. In that, I'm far from alone.

Some male voters have behaved non-consensually themselves, of course, without considering it a big deal. But other men have themselves been recipients of non-consensual touch, and/or have moms, wives, girlfriends, sisters, aunts, daughters, colleagues, and friends in their lives, and would prefer that none of them are ever pussy-grabbed. (Or, as our fierce class of contemporary pundits have noted, they had no particular relationships to specific women to fire them up; they were just raised to be decent humans.)

Some of those latter guys have stepped up as articulate advocates for consent culture. Others simply cannot grasp how common this is. But if there is to be a positive outcome after this nerve- and polity-wracking election cycle, it's grasping what a powerful "Get it all out and heal this shit" moment vis-a-vis rape culture the presidential campaign has been. In 2016, as Kitty was busily assembling this book, Trump by his example made talking about the whole spectrum of sexual assault *fully mainstream.*

One gobsmacking angle of the "Pussygate" discussion has been the right-wing women who insist that, while the rest of us argue that pussy-grabbing is not a character trait we'd like to endorse in our leaders, Trump's real mistake was using such salty verbiage when he talked about his conquests. Men have said this, too—men like Jeff Sessions, in fact—but I've especially noticed female Trump surrogates on this talking point. "Yes," they're essentially saying, "the culture has gotten *shockingly* bad! *Such language!"*

In seeking to understand the mysteries of sex and the conservative mind, we can always count on Rush Limbaugh to boil it down for us. Here's how *he* weighs in on the question of consent. "You know what the magic word, the only thing that matters in American sexual mores today is? One thing. You can do anything—the left will promote and understand and tolerate anything—as long as there is one element. Do you know what it is? Consent. If there is consent on both or all three or all four, however many are involved in the sex act, it's perfectly fine. Whatever it is. But if the left ever senses and smells that there's no consent in part of the equation then here come the rape police. But consent is the magic key to the left."

Limbaugh's message, translated for those who hold San Francisco values: "It's *way* better to engage in a *normal* act non-consensually than to do some pervy thing that everyone enthusiastically consents to." (This reminds me to suggest that none of my young lady friends be alone with Rush Limbaugh. Or—pretty much goes without saying this year—Trump.)

So while I was struggling with writer's block and trying to read the tea leaves of a future that might excuse pussy-grabbing, the outlines of rape culture rose, visible as a breaching whale, from the sea of media coverage. The results of the election exacerbate our fear that rape culture has become more acceptable in the polity, our ability to vanquish it receding, like the white whale, toward the horizon.

At moments like this, of course, the math problem is pretty simple: Redouble our efforts.

My definition of rape culture is a culture that minimizes, ignores, or normalizes acts of sexual non-consent, does not adequately teach about consent, and does not seek to help people learn to pursue their desires in a consensual way. Despite what I said about its genderedness above, as a whole it signifies males (especially cis and heterosexual) as having greater sexual agency than females or people on the trans spectrum, and gives these males more leeway when they exercise this agency. Sexism is the cultural force that genders this: I define that as not believing (or behaving as though) all genders have equal rights and are equally due respect, all the way from providing differential opportunities and benefits, to assuming that someone's value lies in how sexually attractive you feel they are or are not. (All too often, a person's sexual attraction can lead them to problematic conclusions about what the attractive person *is* and *is for*.)

In sex-negative *and* sexist culture you can't be a sexually curious and adventurous woman and be guaranteed respect and safety. This is the heart of the impulse toward slut-shaming. And it's no surprise that slut-shaming has seen a high-profile uptick of late, nor that it has become so politicized. Sex, historically and certainly in a rape-culture context, is *supposed* to be dangerous.

Does this statement seem outrageous to you? Then perhaps you are new to this struggle, or you haven't been paying attention to unwritten but ever-present cultural rules. Sex is *supposed* to be dangerous; this is the way it's always been. This belief explains our culture's problems with reproductive rights, too. Just as the election revealed deep cracks in other progressive gains (racial and LGBT rights are two more of these), we see in the consent-versus-rape-culture struggle a worldview difference that, depending how the die falls, will shape our lives in profoundly different ways. This is a fundamental political question (maybe the very wellspring of "the personal is political"), and will be even if an individual's only use for consent knowledge is to have a more pleasant sex life. But—especially for women and queers—a pleasant sex life has never been a given. Hence both sex information and consent culture are even more political than they appear from the outside.

You can't be any kind of queer, including genderqueer, and be afforded respect and safety across the board. So sex-positivity—not popular culture's "Wheee! Sex!" version, but the *original* definition, which I'll boil down to "Sex is diverse and we all have the right to be ourselves sexually, presuming consent"—is *key* to addressing rape and non-consent. It is the overarching philosophy that states that our sexual desires are our own and can be engaged in, in an atmosphere of consent, any way we choose. Each of us deserves respect, and consensual sexual behavior should never be a source of shame.

To operationalize this set of ideas during this particular historical moment may well feel like the sex and gender version of fighting the Spanish Civil War. The *ancien régime*, the world that until recently we believed we were successfully taking steps to vanquish, has been given new life, a high profile, and a lot of power. On our side of the equation? For one thing, we know that without consent, desire cannot flourish. Without it the structure that allows each human to feel their emotional and erotic life is well-lived is missing, and if the past sixty years have taught us anything it is that that center cannot hold. When sexual experience and exploration were too often laden with shame and opprobrium, we had a sexual revolution; we haven't fully finished it yet. And as we continue this crucial and life-changing work, maybe we should consider it some kind of plus that even Rush Fucking Limbaugh knows that consent is a magic key.

Note: Thanks to Curry College and *Good Vibrations Blog* for the opportunity to develop some of these ideas.

Resources

Books/Essays

These books may offer a useful analysis when discussing consent culture and solutions.

- *Allies in Healing* by Laura Davis
- *Conflict Is Not Abuse* by Sarah Schulman
- *Gift of Fear* by Gavin de Becker
- *Healing Sex* by Staci Haines
- *The Immortal Life of Henrietta Lacks* by Rebecca Skloot
- *Medical Apartheid* by Harriet A. Washington
- *Pagan Consent Culture* by Christine Hoff Kraemer and Yvonne Aburrow
- *The Revolution Starts at Home* edited by Ching-In Chen, Jai Dulani, and Leah Lakshmi Piepzna-Samarasinha

Websites

These websites discuss consent in a variety of ways.

- *Everyday Feminism* – an intersectional, feminist, 101 resource – www.everydayfeminism.com
- *Kink Abuse* – a resource for BDSM and kinky communities about consent and abuse – www.kinkabuse.com
- *Pervocracy* – a kinky, feminist sex blog – www.pervocracy.blogspot.com
- *Meg-John and Justin* – a site packed full of resources discussing consent, particularly around sex – www.megjohnandjustin.com

- *NSPCC* – a UK charity addressing child abuse; the Underwear Rule/Pantosaurus video is useful for explaining boundaries to young children – www.nspcc.org.uk
- *RadTransFem* – a transfeminist gone radical who identifies as an ethical prude – www.radtransfem.wordpress.com
- *Scarleteen* – a website with excellent consent-focused sex education for teens – www.scarleteen.com
- *The Sex Positive Parent* – Airial Clark offers insight and advice on parenting – www.thesexpositiveparent.com
- *Tits and Sass* – written by and for sex workers – www.titsandsass.com
- *Yes Means Yes* – a website continuing the work of the book *Yes Means Yes!* edited by writer and activist Jaclyn Friedman and www.feministing.com founder Jessica Valenti – www. yesmeansyes.com

Crisis Resources

Here are a few support numbers and crisis resources.

- *First Response to Sexual Assault* – tinyurl.com/305lvan
- *Kink Aware Professionals* – tinyurl.com/4c07k3m
- *National Leather Association's Domestic Violence Project* – www.nlaidvproject.us
- *National Domestic Violence Hotline* – 1-800-799-SAFE (1-800-799-7233) or TTY 1-800-787-3224
- *Gay Men's Domestic Violence Project* – www.gmdvp.org, 1-800-832-1901
- *RAINN* (Rape, Abuse and Incest National Network) – www.rainn.org, 1-800-656-HOPE (1-800-656-4673)

Notes

IN THE BEDROOM

The Legal Framework of Consent Is Worthless

Page 15 apps

Jessica Castro. 2016, September 29. "New sexual consent app sparks controversy." *ABC News*. www.abc7news.com/technology/new-sexual-consent-app-sparks-controversy/1532102/

Page 16 Senate Bill No. 967 signed into law

Nick Smith. 2014, September 29. "'Yes Means Yes' California SB 967 Sex Assault Bill Signed by Gov." *ABC News*. www.abc7chicago.com/news/yes-means-yes-california-sb-967-sex-assault-bill-signed/328741/

Page 16 California Education Code, Section 67386

State of California. 2014, February 10. *Senate Bill No. 967, Chapter 748*. www.leginfo.legislature.ca.gov/faces/billNavClient.xhtml?bill_id=201320140SB967

Page 17 attorney Hans Bader

Hans Bader. 2014, June 26. "Senator McCaskill and Obama administration bureaucrats: Most Americans are rapists." *Liberty Unyielding*. www.libertyunyielding.com/2014/06/26/senator-mccaskill-obama-administration-bureaucrats-americans-rapists-sexual-assaulters/

Page 18 BDSM not protected under U.S. law
Neil McArthur. 2016, August 2. "It's a travesty that BDSM isn't technically legal." *Vice*. www.vice.com/en_us/article/its-a-travesty-that-bdsm-isnt-technically-legal

Page 19 Kansas criminalizes deceit when used for the purpose of engaging in sex
Tony Rizzo. 2016, November 3. "Raymore man's arrest puts rape by fraud issue in the spotlight." *Cass County Democrat Missourian*. www.demo-mo.com/2016/11/03/31331/raymore-mans-arrest-puts-rape.html

Page 20 Julio Morales convicted of rape by deceit
Robert J. Lopez. 2014, May 8. "Man gets prison in rape impersonation case that sparked new state law." *Los Angeles Times*. www.latimes.com/local/lanow/la-me-ln-man-gets-prison-rape-impersonation-case-20140508-story.html

Page 20 laws requiring disclosure of a known positive HIV status to sexual partners
Kristena Ducre. 2015, June 22. "It's the law: Disclosing a positive HIV status." *STDcheck.com* [blog]. www.stdcheck.com/blog/hiv-law-disclosure/

Page 21 Kitty Stryker quote
Kitty Stryker. 2015, October 27. "Is it rape?" *purrversatility*. www.kitty-stryker.tumblr.com/post/132026228826/okay-question-is-it-rape-if-when-your-having-sex

Page 22 cheating within a marriage illegal in twenty-one states
Deborah L. Rhode. 2016, May 2. "Why is adultery still a crime?" *Los Angeles Times*. www.latimes.com/opinion/op-ed/la-oe-rhode-decriminalize-adultery-20160429-story.html

Page 23 allegations against Bill Cosby

Kyle Kim, Christina Littlefield, and Mark Olsen. 2016, April 26. "Bill Cosby: A 50-year chronicle of accusations and accomplishments." *Los Angeles Times.* www.latimes.com/ entertainment/la-et-bill-cosby-timeline-htmlstory.html

"Bill Cosby admitted to drugging women to have sex, rape accusers say they are vindicated." 2015, July 7. *Fox News.* www.foxnews.com/entertainment/2015/07/07/bill-cosby-admitted-to-drugging-women-to-have-sex-rape-accusers-say-are.html

Page 23 Brock Turner case

Emanuella Grinberg and Catherine E. Shoichet. 2016, September 2. "Brock Turner released from jail after serving 3 months for sexual assault." *CNN.* www.cnn.com/2016/09/02/us/brock-turner-release-jail/

Page 23 rape kit backlogs

Joyful Heart Foundation. n.d. "What is the rape kit backlog?" *End the backlog* [website]. www.endthebacklog.org/backlog/ what-rape-kit-backlog

Page 23 perpetrators often experience no negative outcomes

RAINN. n.d. "The criminal justice system: Statistics." www.rainn.org/statistics/criminal-justice-system

IN THE SCHOOL

Rehearsing Consent Culture: Revolutionary Playtime

Page 39 *Huffington Post* article
Kate H. 2016, August 17. "An essay on consent, from a woman who
holds huge sex parties." *Huffington Post*. www.huffingtonpost.com/
entry/consent-explained_us_57acdedce4b0e7935e04755a

Page 40 boys and men as primary perpetrators of sexual assault
University of Michigan Sexual Assault Awareness
And Prevention Center. n.d. "Understanding the
perpetrator." www.sapac.umich.edu/article/196

**Page 40 men who sexually assault women often get a mere slap on
the wrist**
Matt Hamilton. 2016, August 30. "Brock Turner to be released from
jail after serving half of six-month sentence in Stanford sexual
assault case." *Los Angeles Times*. www.latimes.com/local/lanow/
la-me-ln-brock-turner-release-jail-20160829-snap-story.html

Page 40 rape culture in college frat houses
Mia de Graaf. 2014, September 22. "Wesleyan University to
end all-male fraternities after two alleged rape cases." *Daily
Mail*. www.dailymail.co.uk/news/article-2765703/Wesleyan-
University-end-male-fraternities-two-alleged-rape-cases.html

Page 40 general resources
Creating Consent Culture: www.creatingconsentculture.com
Incite:www.incite-national.org/page/resources-organizing
Men Stopping Violence: www.menstoppingviolence.org
San Francisco Women Against Rape: www.sfwar.org

Thomas. 2013, October 20. "Cockblocking rapists is a moral
obligation, or, how to stop rape right now." *Yes means yes* [blog].
www.yesmeansyesblog.wordpress.com/2013/10/20/
cockblocking-rapists-is-a-moral-obligation-or-how-to-stop-
rape-right-now
EmilieBuchwald,PamelaFletcher,andMarthaRoth,
eds. 2005. *Transforming a rape culture*. Revised
edition. Minnesota: Milkweed Editions.

IN THE JAIL

Responding to Sexual Harms in Communities: Who Pays and Who Cares?

Page 57 sexual harms in mainstream media and on policy agendas

Paddy Hillyard and Steve Tombs. 2005. "Beyond criminology?"
In Danny Dorling, Dave Gordon, Paddy Hillyard, Christina
Pantazis, Simon Pemberton and Steve Tombs (eds.),
Criminal obsessions: Why harm matters more than crime
(6–23). London: Centre for Crime and Justice Studies.

Page 57 prison industrial complex

Eric A. Stanley and Nat Smith (eds.). 2011. *Captive
genders: Transembodiment and the prison
industrial complex*. Edinburgh: AK Press.

Page 58 sex-critical discourse

Lisa Downing. 2012, July 27. "What is 'sex critical' and why
should we care about it?" *Sex critical: Musings of a curmudgeonly
sexuality studies scholar* [blog]. www. sexcritical.co.uk/ 2012/ 07/
27/what-is-sex-critical-and-why-should-we-care-about-it

Page 58 *The Revolution Starts at Home*

Ching-In Chen, Jai Dulani, and Leah Lakshmi Piepzna-Samarasinha. 2011. *The revolution starts at home: Confronting intimate violence within activist communities.* Brooklyn, NY: South End Press.

Page 59 Kathi Weeks quote

Kathi Weeks. 2011. *The problem with work: Feminism, Marxism, antiwork politics and postwork imaginaries.* London: Duke University Press.

Page 60 *Wages Against Housework*

Silvia Federici. 1975. *Wages against housework.* Bristol: Falling Wall Press.

Page 60 social reproduction

Lise Vogel. 2013. *Marxism and the oppression of women: Towards a unitary theory.* Chicago: Haymarket Press.

Page 61 labor involved in responding to sexual harms

Kathi Weeks. 2011. *The problem with work: Feminism, Marxism, antiwork politics and postwork imaginaries.* London: Duke University Press.

Page 62 care labor

Kathi Weeks. 2011. *The problem with work: Feminism, Marxism, antiwork politics and postwork imaginaries.* London: Duke University Press.

The Kids Aren't All Right: Consent and Our Miranda Rights

Page 66 Miranda for underage persons

Lorelei Laird. 2016, September 21. "Police routinely read juveniles
their Miranda rights, but do kids really understand them?"
American Bar Association [website]. www.americanbar.org/
publications/child_law_practice/vol-35/august-2016/police-
routinely-read-juveniles-their-miranda-rights--but-do-kid.html

Page 67 the dialogue approach

Andrew Guthrie Ferguson. 2012. "The dialogue approach to Miranda
warnings and waiver." *American Criminal Law Review, 49,* 1437.

IN THE HOME

Bodily Autonomy for Kids

Page 109 statistics on child sexual abuse

National Association of Adult Survivors of Child Abuse. n.d.
"What are the statistics of the abused?" www.naasca.org/
2012-Resources/010812-StaisticsOfChildAbuse.htm

Page 112 Lea Grover quote

Lea Grover. 2014, September 8. "This is what sex-positive parenting
really looks like." *Huffington Post.* www.huffingtonpost.com/lea-grover/
this-is-what-sex-positive-parenting-really-looks-like_b_5516707.html

Contributors

AKILAH S. RICHARDS

Akilah S. Richards is a writer, mama, partner, digital nomad, and unschooling activist. She produces podcasts, books, classes, and articles on radical self-expression in practice and in study. Akilah currently facilitates Fare of the Free Child, the only podcast community designed to support, connect, and center People of Color designing their own liberation through Self-Directed Education and love-centered community building at www.akilahrichards.com/podcast.

ALEX DYMOCK

Alex Dymock is a lecturer in criminology and law at Royal Holloway, University of London. Alex's research is primarily in the areas of gender, sexuality, and criminal justice. She has published previously on issues surrounding consent in BDSM relationships, the commodification of kink, and the politics and aesthetics of pornography.

AV FLOX

AV Flox is a freelance journalist who writes about the intersection of sex, law, and technology.

CAMERYN MOORE

Image: Caleb Cole

Cameryn Moore is an award-winning playwright and performer, a sex activist and educator, a sidewalk pornographer, and a long-time phone sex operator. Her work in theater, literature, activism, and advocacy is both a challenge and an invitation to adventurous audiences everywhere. She is the writer and performer of five solo shows: *Phone Whore*, *slut (r)evolution*, *for | play*, *The Pretty One (and other things that need to be said)*, and *nerdfucker*. To date, she has toured these shows to over 50 cities around North America and the United Kingdom. She is the creator and frequent host of Smut Slam, a storytelling open mic featuring real-life, first-person sex stories, and BEDx, a bar education night for sex geeks. When not performing, Cameryn sets up her world-famous traveling Smut Stand, providing bespoke typewritten erotica on the spot to happy drunks and discerning passersby. She is frequently NSFW on Facebook; you can also keep up with her at www.camerynmoore.com.

CAROL QUEEN

A noted cultural sexologist whose work has been widely published, Queen has written or co-edited several books, including the influential *PoMoSexual* and *Real Live Nude Girl: Chronicles of Sex-Positive Culture*. She has been speaking publicly about sexuality for over 40 years; she frequently speaks at colleges as well as to general and specialized audiences. Queen co-founded the Center for Sex and Culture (www.sexandculture.org) in San Francisco and is staff sexologist and company historian at Good Vibrations, the women-founded sex shop, where she has worked since 1990. She is the lead author on *The Sex & Pleasure Book: Good Vibrations Guide to Great Sex for Everyone.*

CHERRY ZONKOWSKI

Cherry Zonkowski is a Bay Area–based writer, storyteller, and performer. Her one-woman show *Reading My Dad's Porn and French Kissing the Dog* was a hit at the Marsh Theater, and she is the author of *Cheeky Tiki Bang Gang: The Case of the Creepy Christian Camp.*

CINNAMON MAXXINE

Cinnamon Maxxine is a Bay Area–born and raised original warrior diva. Unfortunately, due to capitalism, racism, and just all around bullshit, they're growing more and more salty and bitter every day. Although they are always all smiles and full of laughter, the terrible shit you perpetuate in the world is killing Cinnamon.

EVE RICKERT AND FRANKLIN VEAUX

Eve Rickert and Franklin Veaux are the coauthors of *More Than Two: A Practical Guide to Ethical Polyamory*. Franklin is the creator of the website www.morethantwo.com and the author of the *The Game Changer: A Memoir of Disruptive Love*. Eve and Franklin live in Vancouver, Canada.

JETTA RAE

Jetta Rae runs the food blog *Fry Havoc* and spends most of her free time playing ukulele and falling in and out of love with various pinball machines.

JIZ LEE

Jiz Lee has worked in the adult industry for over a decade, spanning independent erotic films and hardcore gonzo pornography. A versatile performer and key player in the queer porn movement, Jiz has received numerous industry nods and was honored by The Trans 100. (Jiz is nonbinary and uses the gender-neutral pronouns they/them.) Besides working behind the scenes at Pink and White Productions (www.crash-padseries.com, www.pinklabel.tv), they've also presented at academic institutions such as Princeton University and at the American Studies Association Conference, and have appeared on MSNBC and the BBC. They have also been a contributor to *The Feminist Porn Book* and *Global Information Society Watch: Sexual Rights and the Internet* and co-edited the *Porn Studies* journal special issue *Porn and Labour*. Their first book, *Coming Out Like a Porn Star*, is the largest collection of essays written by porn professionals.

JOELLEN NOTTE

JoEllen is a writer, speaker, researcher, and mental health advocate. Since 2012 she has written about sex, vibrators, mental health, and how none of us are broken on her award-winning site, *The Redhead Bedhead*. JoEllen has led workshops on sexual communication, navigating consent, having casual sex kindly, and dating as an introvert. She has toured sex shops, spoken at length on dildos, and founded a center for sex education, but she is happiest and most effective when writing and speaking on behalf of quiet people who have sex—check out her video series on attending conferences as an introvert and extensive writing on sex and depression. JoEllen is certified as a sex educator through the Planned Parenthood League of Massachusetts Sexuality Education Certification Series and has spoken at Clark College, the University of Chicago, Woodhull's Sexual Freedom Summit, and the Playground Conference.

KATE FRACTAL

Kate Fractal is a professional educator in the Boston area. She has been involved in the local theater-style live-action roleplaying (LARP) community for over ten years as a player. Kate also runs games and wrote the LARP *Afterparty*, which was nicknamed "Sexual Identity: The LARP" by players.

KITTY STRYKER

Kitty Stryker is a writer, activist, and authority on developing a consent culture in alternative communities. She was the founder of www.consentculture.com, a hub for LGBT, kinky, and polyamorous folks looking for a sex-critical approach to relationships. Kitty also cofounded the artsy sexy party Kinky Salon London, as well as co-founding Struggalo Circus, being active with the NorCal Degendettes, and acting as head of cosplay for queer gaming convention GaymerX. Kitty tours internationally, speaking at universities and conferences about feminism, sex work, body positivity, queer politics, and more. She lives in Oakland, California, with her cat Foucault.

LAURA KATE DALE

Equal parts LGBT+ rights critic and video game reviewer. Editor-in-chief at *Let's Play Video Games*. Freelancer at *Polygon*; *Rock, Paper, Shotgun*; the *Guardian*; *Kotaku*; and *Vice*. Talks a lot online about being a gay trans woman working in tech.

LAURIE PENNY

Image: Nadya Lev

Laurie Penny is a writer, journalist, and feminist activist from London. She is the author of seven books, including *Unspeakable Things* (Bloomsbury, 2014) and *Bitch Doctrine* (Bloomsbury, 2017).

NAVARRE OVERTON

Navarre Overton is a writer from Minneapolis, Minnesota. She writes on a variety of topics from a feminist and social justice lens.

PORSCHA COLEMAN

Porscha Coleman is a writer and poet based in the Washington, DC, area. Porscha specializes in intersections of race, gender, sexuality, and mental health in popular culture and can be contacted through her website, www.porschalcoleman.com.

RICHARD M. WRIGHT

Richard M. Wright is a Jamaican New Yorker who currently lives in Florida. He studied expressive arts therapy at the California Institute of Integral Studies, where he obtained his MA. Richard has also done healthy masculinity and bystander intervention training with Men Can Stop Rape, and he uses both of these trainings to cocreate consent culture with youth in middle schools and high schools. He believes that, more than ever, it is important to support healthy, accountable, liberatory masculinities; consent culture; and the lives and voices of women, girls, and feminine folk of all genders. Richard is also a visual artist, a DJ, and a soon-to-be-published writer of afrofuturist/visionary fiction. He weaves themes of consent culture and liberation into those modalities as well. He is honored to contribute to this anthology, and wishes for the messages within to go far and wide.

ROZ KAVENEY

Roz Kaveney describes herself as an elderly novelist and poet living in London. She says that she is not really an activist these days.

SEZ THOMASIN

Sez Thomasin is an autistic, genderqueer poet and sex educator from Yorkshire, England. Their limericks on the subject of gender identity have been featured in *My New Gender Workbook* by Kate Bornstein. Sez lives with their wife and a delinquent cat in Sheffield.

SHAWN D. TAYLOR

Shawn. D. Taylor tells stories. Sometimes on the page, sometimes live and in person, sometimes on film, and sometimes in an audio recording. He tells stories because he is nosy (curious) about how we move and make sense of our shared world. Shawn has a couple of books published, a sporadic podcast, and tons of his writing can be found online.

TAKEALLAH RIVERA

A full-spectrum doula, educator, writer, and mother, Takeallah Rivera is a southern-born feminist activist and outspoken introvert. She is passionate about reproductive justice, postpartum mental health awareness, marine biology, coffee, and mimosas. She boasts a BA in education and too many certifications to fit on her résumé, including certifications as a mental health peer support specialist and breastfeeding peer counselor. When she isn't providing doula support at Make Lemonade Full Spectrum Doula Services, she is serving her community as a middle school educator and pet sitter at Canine to Five.

TOBI HILL-MEYER

Whether crafting policy, speaking at colleges, leading lobbying efforts, or making porn, Tobi Hill-Meyer is a powerhouse of activity dedicated to ending oppression and supporting the trans community, with a special focus on trans feminism, trans health, and sexuality.

VIRGIE TOVAR

Virgie Tovar is an author, an activist, and one of the nation's leading experts and lecturers on fat discrimination and body image. She the creator of Babecamp, a four-week online course for women who are ready to break up with diet culture. She also started the hashtag campaign #LoseHateNotWeight. Tovar edited the groundbreaking anthology *Hot & Heavy: Fierce Fat Girls on Life, Love & Fashion.*

ZEV UBU HOFFMAN

Zev Ubu Hoffman is a board member of a thriving sex-positive nonprofit in the Bay Area. Over the last eight years, Zev has helped cultivate enthusiastic consent–focused communities throughout the Bay Area. He is a prolific artist and accomplished communicator.

He has submerged himself within a diverse set of communities, from BDSM-oriented to costumed Dadaesque poly communities, as well as lifestyle swingers, and the many communities that lie in the cross-sections. These experiences have given him an innate understanding of the diverse nature of cultivating consent culture within human sexuality.

Index

W

Weeks, Kathi, 59, 61, 62. *see also* care labor

wrestling

 as a collaboration, 137, 139

 and consent, 136–37, 138

 as dangerous, 135, 138, 139

Y

"yes means yes," 13, 16–17, 57. *see also* Senate
  Bill 967 ("yes means yes" law)

Z

zemiology, 57